For Grandy and Pops

Without you, none of this

Contact information for Arrowhead Road Publishing—P.O. Box 462, Littleton, CO 80126

ARROWHEAD ROAD
P U B L I S H I N G

ISBN: 979-8-218-02048-4 (paperback)
ISBN: 979-8-218-02049-1 (ebook)

Ordering Information:
Special discounts are available on quantity purchases by corporations, associations, and others. For details, contact www.creativeadventurefamily.com

CREATIVE ADVENTURING

BY
JONATHAN BITZ

WITH
**GEMMA, SILAS, AND
HARLOW BITZ**

EDITED BY
KELSEY BOWE

TABLE OF CONTENTS

CREATIVE ADVENTURING

A FIELD GUIDE FOR AN INSPIRED LIFE

A PARENTING PARADIGM FUELED BY CHILD-LEAD LEARNING AND EXPLORATION

BY
JONATHAN BITZ

WITH
**GEMMA, SILAS, AND
HARLOW BITZ**

EDITED BY
KELSEY BOWE

CHAPTER ONE

A NEW WAY OF LIFE

"Inside all of us is fear. Inside all of us is adventure. Inside all of us is … A Wild Thing."
— Maurice Sendak

I remember standing at the kitchen sink one day in 2019, after our third baby was born, and thinking, "This is not how I want to live." I was so empty and tired of the cycle: waking up at all hours of the night, poopy diapers, pee in the beds, vomit, breakfast, cleaning, school, lunch, cleaning, crying, naps, more crying, more poop, more tears, more food, more messes, baths, reading, cleaning up, bedtime. Thinking of the next decade of this repetition exhausted me even more.

I knew something needed to be done to break this cycle of mundanity that was breaking me. It was breaking all of us—and had been for generations.

I started putting together lists of museums, parks, hiking trails, natural wonders, and day trips, anything we could do to change things up, to activate our potential, and to give us something to look forward to outside the grind of daily life.

We all needed it. We needed to be injected with some inspiration, with daily meaning and creative goals, not just living for getting to the end of the day without a calamity. Living is different from surviving.

The hectic schedule of owning two businesses in addition to caring for three young children took a toll on my marriage, and my wife and I slowly lost our connection and sense of partnership. I found myself fighting to keep us together, but really I was just fighting to live the kind of life I had always wanted, the kind of life that was inspired and interesting.

Because I believed it was possible—I just didn't know how to live that kind of life.

But I knew one thing was certain: the babies deserved it.

The babies, as I have called them for so long, are now toddlers: Gemma, the older sister, is six years old. Silas Sawyer is four. Harlow Bear is two.

Sometimes the Hardest Thing Is the Best Thing

Then, a divorce happened.

It was the hardest thing I've ever done. It's the hardest thing I'm still doing, over two years removed from the day that I left my family's home for good—the same day we sold my dream, my business. The timing was unspeakably brutal, and I felt composed fully of loss and heartache. But beneath the feeling of having lost everything at once was the deeper knowledge held by the fallow earth in winter: that the inevitable spring holds a garden of possibilities, new growth, and new brambles to tend or let run wild.

How could I hold myself accountable? How could I reconcile my past choices with whom I wanted myself to be? And how can I best exemplify that ideal for my children? After all, they are impressions of who I am, where I came from, and where I am going. We had a fresh start, and we could live in any way we wanted to.

That was it. This was the imperative, the fresh start. It was time to change our mindset as a family. It was also time for me to change my mindset as a father and to embody the spirit of leadership I know has always been within me, the leadership that dwells within us all.

I was determined to change our lives, our direction, our swagger and style, and our outlook. I intended to infuse our lives with meaning.

I wanted virtues exemplified. A family crest. Cohesion. Direction. Inspiration. Adventure.

I wanted a new life, but I wasn't sure how to go about creating it. Still, through the darkest night of my life, with the support and grace of family and friends, we both gradually and immediately started to shape a new vision together.

Curses Become Blessings

We got one long summer together to learn how to live the life I wanted us to always live.

I took the babies to every museum we have in town. We moved to an area laced with great parks and paths and pools and creeks and open spaces.

We created a scooter gang. My posse and I packed lunches and hit the sidewalks and trails. We came home sunburnt for the boys' afternoon naps. After we ate supper, we rode into the sunset and came back after dark.

And I relished stepping into the archetypal role of the hero, finding things we lost in the journey—like my five-year-old's lost Barbie shoe—somewhere in the nighttime mile behind us. I'll never forget my daughter exclaiming over and over that first time: "Dada, you get five congratulations!"

It felt as if we were finally doing something. The scooter wheels were churning toward the horizons of our design.

Then winter came. We went indoors, and with the help of my

mother and father, we found new tools for the kids to stay inspired and educated and growing.

I was hungry for more outings with them. I wanted them to continue to have exciting days with me.

Then, COVID-19.

All of a sudden, the spring we were all looking forward to no longer existed. We couldn't go back to the playgrounds. We couldn't go back to the museums. We learned a lesson about expectations.

I had to discover some other way, without predesigned amusements or curricula.

Or rather, I had to let this other way discover me.

In the natural flow of our life, an organic mindset started emerging: *let's go*. Let's go on adventures. We still can.

The novel coronavirus forced me to become more creative, more novel.

What initially felt like yet another curse blossomed into a moment of profound blessing; this was the precise mountain that I needed to climb.

Instead of relying on the basics like playgrounds and pools and public places, we leaned into the natural world. We started finding places to go where nobody was. Turns out, there's a lot of places where nobody is, where kids can find exactly what they need.

With no school for the kids to go to, I started putting lesson plans together on what was around us: the robin and its nest outside the window, the lilacs at the mansion that we picnicked at, snails, toads, and the raptors we delighted in locating, as they soared overhead.

At this point, my babies can identify more flowers, plants, and animals than I could as a teenager. Why? Because we creatively adventure. We go out and explore. We go inward and explore.

The Spirit of Creative Adventuring

It wasn't explicit, but I just started calling our outings "adventures." Instead of going to the museum, or the park, or riding scooters, we started saying, "Let's go on an adventure."

It stuck.

Slowly, it started to become something. A thing. Our thing. It became our cabal, our thriving slice inside the universe where we were always safe.

Of course, I conceptualized the safety of it all, the bubble. I'll admit that I almost became addicted to it: It was the space and time when my life of starting over washed away and we were all just simply together, the four of us, paying attention. We were adventuring.

Preparation is essential. Every adventure starts with getting three toddlers dressed appropriately and making lunch. Our backpacks are stocked with essentials; our bodies are outfitted correctly. I get them all in the car, buckled, calm, and ready for a little drive. Then, onward.

But even when it was hard, and at times it is very difficult with three babies—for them and for me—you break through, and it's worth it.

We were finding things: new places, new creeks, new sunsets, and new, secret places that we felt as if we were the first explorers in.

We were always on the hunt for things: heart-shaped rocks, rocks to build cairns, bugs, feathers, nests fallen from trees, or bones.

In each new environment, the kids lead the way. It's my responsibility to springboard off their natural curiosity. And really, it's easy. Natural curiosity both intrigues me and fuels my daily life. It always has. So, I just need to do what's natural to me and respond to their natural instincts. And thus, I become a curator, of their outings, of their days, of their lives.

They lead. I follow.

It can be as simple as them noticing some large rodents on the ranch we passed.

"What are those?"

"Prairie dogs," I replied.

They'd try to sound out that strange word, "prairie."

And so, for the rest of the afternoon, we'd be on the lookout for prairie dogs. It would only, in this instance, be a minor embellishment to our afternoon, but an emphasis nevertheless. For when we returned home, I'd pull up some videos about prairie dogs' dens and way of life.

We don't go on "hikes." We don't go on "walks." We don't just get on our scooters and ride because of this mindset. No, we're simply going on adventures, creatively. And the difference? It's gigantic.

The difference is gigantic because we control all the variables that we can. We control the goals and the mindset of meaning, and as a result, we manage to stay in our little fantastic, magical bubble where the things we want to happen manifest their way into our existence.

Eureka!

It's more about ethos and perspective than anything. But the moment it all clicked for me was one evening when the babies and I were on a little creek called Sand Creek, the name of the creek that made my Silas's namesake famous.

They were scared. There was debris from previous floods blocking our way. There were spiders. Snakes.

My five-year-old said, "Dad, I think this is a bad idea."

The looks on my boys' faces, aged three and one, told me the same thing.

Then we overcame a few big obstacles. Then they started to learn how to navigate the stream, how to locate and then take the easiest route. They learned how to keep their feet under them on the mossy rocks. They learned how to move through the buckwheat and foxtail.

Slowly, they gained confidence.

I was nervous, as I sometimes still am on our adventures: that I'm leading them the wrong way, that I'm pushing them too hard, or that they just aren't ready for this … yet. I'm still learning to balance fear and trust. I'm preparing them as I prepare us.

Then to my surprise, my three-year-old, who was struggling most of the time, full of fear, took the lead of our expedition. I didn't see it happen until he let me know.

"Look, Dad, I'm the leader now!"

And then one of the most profound things that I've ever been a part of happened out of the clear ether of the moment. It was pure magic.

My three-year-old kept exclaiming: "*I can do it!* Look, Dad, I'm doing it!"

Suddenly his whole being expanded with light and courage, and he was suddenly just bigger, navigating waterfalls and bank drops and foxtails and horsetails, in and out of the creek.

"I am doing it! Dad, I can do it!"

I was so choked up, I almost failed to respond. I could only howl. It's something we still do: *howl.*

Doing it he was. We all were—swelling, embracing, and embraced.

And our life of creative adventuring was born.

I've always known what I wanted. It's always been the same: an inspired life, an interesting life.

Now, this has become the explicit way I've long wanted to live. It has always remained ineffable, but now it has become framed within the ecstatic momentum of the present. We all have visions for living the life we want, but sometimes we don't have the words, the package. That doesn't mean we still can't embody that *feeling* of boundless life with courage.

Not until just recently did I understand, more succinctly, what that life really looks and sounds like. It sounds like laughter amid silence. It looks like my children stepping into *themselves* as they step into the creek.

Now I have this incredible and powerful phrase that has been clarified, because I started finally living, not just surviving, alongside my family. This idea has changed everything: creative adventuring.

The Coauthors, the Babies, my Children

I thought you should know who we're talking about here, these amazing creatures, my coconspirators, my adventure tribe. So, I put together a little introduction:

Gemma is a precocious first grader. She is, as I call her, the most beautiful girl in the world. She has an amazing memory. She loves painting and drawing and everything Barbie. Fashion is of high intrigue for her. She turns on the sun in every room she enters. She is a parent to two, Julie and Grace—her American Girl dolls.

Silas Sawyer was named after one of my heroes, the abolitionist and Colorado Civil War hero, Silas Stillman Soule.[1] Silas is special. He's magical. Fiery. Sensitive. Strong, so strong physically. It was he who was probably affected the most from the transition into our new life. For a while it was dark, but he's walked back into the light. He's back to laughing and building Magna-Tiles and Legos and crafting and drawing and obsessing about (and then playing) Roblox. Si loves snakes and skeletons.

Harlow Bear, two years old at the time of writing, is the best cuddler in the world. He gives great Bear kisses and huge Bear hugs. Every morning when they're with me, he's the last thing I see before I sleep and the first thing I see when I wake. He is passionate about all construction vehicles, motorcycles, and fast cars, and when Bear is in the car, we brake for big, big rigs, trains, and every blue and orange vehicle.

---

1 "Silas Soule (1838–1865)," Genealogy, African American & Western History Resources, Denver Public Library, accessed May 13, 2022, https://history.denverlibrary.org/colorado-biographies/silas-soule-1838-1865.

CHAPTER TWO

WHAT IS CREATIVE ADVENTURING?

Creative adventuring is a general mode of living that I've adapted to become a parenting approach in which I take the mundane and pivot it into a magical and expansive experience for my kids.

They are the ones who typically lead me to these discoveries, these openings, these "door-adjacents." My kids lead and live, and I pay attention, follow, and then curate our experiences together. This often happens spontaneously, and experience itself then becomes our teacher.

I love the historicity of words. It provides so much insight. Our favorite word, you may have noticed, is "adventure"; its etymology illuminates the properties that excite me about this mode of living, and it really brings this paradigm to life.

The word "adventure" finds its origins in 12th- and 13th-century words that mean "to risk the loss of," "risk and danger," or "a perilous undertaking." And last, it also means "a novel or exciting incident, a remarkable occurrence in one's life."[2]

What struck me in this etymology was this idea of "risking

---

2 Online Etymology Dictionary, s.v. "venture (v.)," accessed May 13, 2022, https://www.etymonline.com/word/venture.

the loss of." What are we losing? A hackneyed, prosaic experience, that's what we're losing.

What a big idea.

In order to achieve the annihilation of the banal, there is risk: the kids' safety. There is risk in the fact that my idea for an adventure will fail. Oh, and they have. I have failed. A few adventures turned out to be duds. With some, the creek was flowing too high to cross, so we had to abandon the entire outing. Another time, I forgot bug repellent, and the kids were devoured by giant mosquitos. Many other times, the kids didn't enjoy the lesson plans I put together and yawned through them all.

So, a new mode of operation rose to the surface: go with the flow. Be water. We won't always succeed. Scrap it and adjust and edit and move toward something else.

But whatever you do: be water.

Perhaps this is the biggest lesson at the core of creative adventuring: malleability. Edit life. Be nonattached. Move on. Manage expectations, and embrace the unexpected.

I'm interested in calculated risk. I'm not interested in endangering the kids any more than I feel comfortable with. We've backed off several paths and streams and adventures that were simply just not safe enough.

We don't need Mount Everest to satiate our thirst for experience. We do, however, build little Everests all over the place.

And we do that because we put ourselves out there. Adventuring with three toddlers is hard. It takes a lot to load up and take off. I mostly carry Bear, my two-year-old, on my shoulders. It's tiring, and rocks are slippery, and I have to be extra cautious with him up there. Then they play in the mud and water, eat lunch, make a mess, and then up he goes, back onto my shoulders, his wet, sticky pants rubbing on my face and neck. It takes even more to come back home all sandy and muddy and tired, get their clothes off, and get them bathed.

But when we all go to bed exhausted and sore, I know that we achieved something special. Will they remember it a decade from now? I'm not so sure. But I am certain that we accomplished that primary goal of creating a "novel or exciting incident, a remarkable occurrence in one's life."

"And above all, watch with glittering eyes the whole world around you because the greatest secrets are always hidden in the most unlikely places.

Those who don't believe in magic will never find it."
— Roald Dahl, *The Minpins*[3]

Safe Is Not Commensurate with Being

I hear it all the time when I tell our loved ones what we're doing or where we're going: "Be safe!"

The word "safe" comes from a 14th- and 15th-century word that means "not exposed to danger" and "free from risk."[4]

As far as I am employing this model in my parenting, I need to emphasize as I do often with those in my life: I don't have children; I have babies. My kiddos are six, four, and two years old. Realistically we should identify them as toddlers, or kids. But to me, they're babies. And I love that they are identified as such because my big heart knows this won't last for long.

We're not going rock climbing, bouldering, or on any mountaineering expeditions. In fact, I'm not interested in looking at any of this through those traditional lenses (more on that later).

---

3 Roald Dahl, *The Minpins* (New York: Viking Books for Young Readers, 1991).

4 Online Etymology Dictionary, s.v., "safe (adj.)," accessed May 13, 2022, https://www.etymonline.com/word/safe.

For now—safety. With babies, there's always a risk, especially in the wild and especially with babies who can't swim or fend off a snake or find their way home if lost.

We went to the ocean for their first time, and even that, standing in the crashing waves on Laguna Beach, is dangerous.

It's up to me, as Dada, to not just protect them but to put them in situations that they're leery of—in a calculated manner.

At first, at the ocean, they were terrified. So was I. I knew the risks, and after being away from the ocean for so long, you forget how powerful those waves are and how quickly something can go wrong. So, with my brother and his wife, we created protocols: Eyes are always on the kids. You watch him; I'll watch her. Tell me when we need to switch.

The axiom I've long lived with is "Nothing great was ever achieved in comfort." And there is no such thing as guaranteed safety.

I grew up with an adventurous family. My best friend to this day, Daniel, has lived a long life full of outdoor adventures that started when his mother's water broke while she was fishing with his father on the Arkansas River, on the day he was born.

Daniel's advice on taking my babies into the wild was that in the exploration of the unknown, you don't control nature. A good adventurer knows and prepares for this. Controls you may have on your side can disappear in an instant.

But, as he said, "To have gone out and taken a risk in that unknown, and gained and lost, is an adventure; that is from where stories are told."

Creative Adventuring Isn't Just About the Outdoors

It's not.

Again, it's about a mode of living and the boundlessness of our imagination.

Sure, we can go to the creeks, which are our favorite, or to the mountains. We can be on trails where we live in Colorado in under an hour. We can catch toads and frogs and pretty beetles. We've caught snails—that was their first pet until the snails bred and made over 20 babies. We pick lilac flowers and make jam. We explore for bones and sightings of raptors and raptor nests. We are always on the hunt for our favorite flowers, the oft-elusive Colorado state flower, the blue columbine.

But we also make DIY Barbie clothes. My six-year-old does Kumon, a unique educational method to help accelerate children's learning. We've just started the family band. We paint rocks. We have a huge craft table that the kids love to build and paint and draw on. I create drawings of them as their favorite superheroes for them to color. We create educational tools so they can learn to count money and trace letters that spell their names.

Creative Adventuring Means Step It Up

As their father, I am responsible for guiding them and supporting them. In this paradigm of adventuring, it's also my responsibility to get inventive, to find activities for them to engage in that are nourishing, fresh, and provocative.

This mode of living puts pressure on me to take the time and the effort, to learn new skills like how to make lilac jelly, how to draw better, or how to create a lesson around whatever interests them at the moment—whether that's the satellite dishes by our house, Bigfoot, llamas, alpacas, frogs, dinosaurs, ghosts, or whatever. It forces me to educate myself so that I can share appropriate material with them.

All of this forces me to be a better parent, to truly listen to the guiding voices of my children, and, moreover, to be a better man, to be the kind of man I always wanted to be.

This is a portrait of the parent as active, engaged, and aware.

For me, the idea of creative adventuring is the panacea for harmful parenting pitfalls, such as helicopter parenting. Instead, through a balance of boundaries, caution, and freedom, we cultivate emotional intelligence. We practice overcoming adversity. Through openness and preparedness, we all learn to adapt and harness the beauty of our world and our humanity.

But to do that, I've learned that you must be willing to set your ego to the side. You must be willing to be injected with a little fear. You must face risk. Life is a risk.

Otherwise, why would you do this at all?

Answer—because the rewards are simply too great to not risk

the loss of old maps and old ideas that were never working for us anyway.

Creative adventuring is the act of letting go.

CHAPTER THREE

CORE VALUES

Be Curious

This is the cornerstone of our paradigm. I think it should be the cornerstone for all early educational models; for if you instill the power of curiosity, students become lifetime learners. And when they do that, they organically acquire the necessary skills to move forth in a progressive and wonder-bound way.

What curiosity yields is an ecstatic understanding. This type of cognition is one of the primary human motivations and fills in the landscape where ecstasy lives.

Jason Silva defines cognitive ecstasy as "an exhilarating neural storm of intense intellectual pleasure."[5]

This exhilaration occurs when we connect patterns—to do so is one of the delights of the mind. This process is something that children experience … a lot.

To be curious is an ancient, primal, and childlike quality. It's often trained out of us through acculturation. It's something seen as an interference in the social world: "See, she can't sit still. She's always distracted by things. She probably has ADHD."

What if, instead of that, we took a counterintuitive route and said: "She's very curious about a lot of things, and she's maybe

---

5   Jason Silva: Shots of Awe, "The Ecstasy of Curiosity," YouTube video, 3:13, September 16, 2014, https://www.youtube.com/watch?v=VOVmVMJEhg8.

overwhelmed with curiosity right now. Watch her. We should help her navigate her wonderment."

If you instill curiosity and the sense of wonder and mystery and adventure into learning, education then moves out of the factory of the public school and into the realm of magic and exploration, along with all the great books, films, songs, and virtues of higher consciousness.

I have long believed that if we instill curiosity in our children, everything else will fall into place.

In a 2019 study titled "Within-Person Variability in Curiosity During Daily Life and Associations with Well-Being," researchers Lydon-Staley, Zurn, and Bassett explored the correlation between curiosity and well-being.[6]

What did they find? Curiosity blunts depressed mood and encourages physical activity. In summary, curiosity creates happiness. And happiness creates an ability to be more curious. They go hand in hand. They nourish each other.

Curiosity is an active function. In order to be curious, one must be in movement. More than that, one must not be afraid of that movement.

In trying to define curiosity, I like Lydon-Staley, Zurn, and Bassett's definition. They, piggybacking on other researchers' work, state: "Curiosity is the propensity to seek out novel, complex, and challenging interactions with the world (Kashdan & Steger, 2007; Loewenstein, 1994). Curiosity facilitates engagement with unfamiliar information (Silvia, 2008), even if that in formation challenges existing beliefs and instills uncertainty" (Kashdan et al., 2009).[7]

Curiosity is synthesis. Curiosity is dynamic.

---

6 David Lydon-Staley et al., "Within-Person Variability in Curiosity During Daily Life and Associations with Well-Being," *Journal of Personality* 88, no. 4 (2020): 625–641, https://doi.org/10.1111/jopy.12515.

7 Lydon-Staley et al., "Within-Person Variability," 625–641.

Curiosity is a process. To be curious is to challenge existing beliefs that are yours and most of which are not yours. Curiosity is not an end goal. It's not a neatly drawn X on any map.

Curiosity is the road and the path and the journey. To exist in a state of inquisition is its own challenge and reward.

As is the case with love, being curious isn't a given. It's not just one thing, one sensation, or one drive. It's a nexus of many different skills.

Being curious means you will end up in unknown places and new situations. In other words, being curious is an undertaking. And with every experiment, every adventure, comes the risk of failure.

To be good at being curious you must first be good at failing.

Flow State

Flow state is the goal.

Flow state is when you feel amazing and when you are able to do amazing things.

Sometimes we call it "the zone."

Jason Silva defines it with an acronym: STER.

STER stands for:

Selflessness

Your sense of self vanishes. The dorsal lateral prefrontal cortex—the part of the brain responsible for all that monkey chatter, the self-conscious editor in your brain all the time—goes quiet. Flow state is the ultimate presence experienced without a sense of self, without a sense of ego. It's agelessness.

Timelessness

Time becomes wonky. It can speed up or slow way, way down.

Effortlessness

Your actions don't require effort or push or pull. They just … flow.

Richness

You are privy to more information and data.[8]

Performance and risk and lateral thinking all increase while you're in flow.

Flow is the ideal human state.

So how do we get there? You need to find what triggers you and what triggers your children.

Silva, an expert on flow state, says that universal flow triggers all require a little novelty (curiosity) and risk (adventure).

Adversity

The point is not to lessen fear but to become more courageous.

This is another central value to creative adventuring. To adventure creatively also means to adventure bravely.

Simply put, things are not always going to work out. If you master this, you will master yourself. And if you don't master yourself, somebody else, or something else, will master you.

To be good at failing, you must understand your emotions. This is one of the core goals as a creatively adventuring parent: teaching and embodying emotional intelligence.

I will explain the techniques that I've learned about this for little ones and big ones alike a bit later on.

Be a Lifetime Learner

Believing that "curiosity is the propensity to seek out novel, complex, and challenging interactions with the world" means that one must possess the ability to cope with change.

The world is in motion. At times we get stuck in a bubble, and things appear stagnant.

---

8 Jason Silva, "Selflessness, Timelessness, Effortlessness, Richness.... this is FLOW," Facebook, July 2, 2017, video, 2:29, https://www.facebook.com/jasonlsilva/posts/selflessness-timelessness-effortlessness-richness-this-is-flow/1874656286131981/?_rdr.

At times we feel stuck, even bored.

But the truth is that the world is in motion. Life is about motion. Everything changes. Objects and ideas aren't things—rather they are processes. Everything is in motion.

It's difficult to remember moments of triumph, to encourage the kids to remember when they were successful, why they were successful, and what it took to succeed in something. What is demonstrated here is that fundamental presupposition: Everything is in motion. Here, the idea is that success is about being in motion and going with the current of life and challenges, not resisting it.

Teach your children how to be lifelong learners who

- seek out novel situations, locating them, confronting them, and then handling them,
- appreciate *subtle* novelty and nuances and find wonder in the mundane,
- open gaps, instead of closing them,
- intentionally create discomfort,
- acknowledge that negative emotions exist to try to protect them from something and know how to transmute those scary emotions into positivity,
- move forward with new personal insights instead of getting mired in the negative, and
- evoke curiosity.

Be Inspired

Inspiration is creativity in motion.

The qualities work together in symbiosis. By engaging in creative pursuits, you're welcoming inspiration to arrive. And by welcoming inspiration to arrive, you're therefore already in an organically creative state of exploration and adventure.

Psychologists Todd M. Thrash and Andrew J. Elliot have found that inspiration consists of three main qualities:

- **Evocation**
  It's evoked spontaneously, without your control.
- **Approach motivation**
  It gives one the feeling that you must make your vision happen in that instant.
- **Transcendence**
  It gives one the sense of clarity and single-mindedness when the rest of your life fades away and you're present in that moment and inspired.[9]

Profound inspiration means that you are both inspired by something and, at the same time, inspired to do something.

The thing is, inspiration just happens. But it's about putting yourself, or your children, in the position of inviting innovation to appear in each moment.

Researchers believe there are a couple of ways to do this.

One way is to be open to experience. You need to accept the consequences of your engagement, the risk, as opposed to trying to control your children and trying to make them fit some prescribed mold. You need to go with the flow of the moment and the flow of them, the actors in this play.

Another way is to be intrinsically motivated, not extrinsically. The motivation must come from inside you—not because of something, like a reward that exists outside of you. This is also to say that simply being inspired is its own reward.

Another way is to cultivate skills enough so that you have

9   Todd Thrash and Andrew Elliot, "Inspiration as a Psychological Construct," *Journal of Personality and Social Psychology* 84, no. 4 (2003): 871–889, https://doi.org/10.1037/0022-3514.84.4.871.

enough mastery to put yourself in a position of breaking through to an inspired place. Master painters are more able to put themselves into a space of inspirational breakthrough quicker and more often than novices. Practice does indeed make perfect.

Inspiration is spontaneous. But by cultivating other skills of exploration and work mastery, you invite its presence into your daily life and the lives of your children.

Agnosia

I am agnostic. And no, I don't just mean spiritually or religiously.

I believe this is one of the cornerstones for curiosity and exploration: *to not know.*

"Agnosia," from Greek, means a special kind of knowledge, a dark knowledge. More than that, this is where a knowledge of the big things like God resides. This actually may be one of the places where the Christian idea of faith comes from, from a 14th-century text on the great cloud of unknowing.

"Agnosia" is often construed as a lack of knowledge. I do not believe in that pejorative interpretation. For me, in this place of unknowing, this is where all the magic and all the knowledge actually comes to us from.

As with the other core values, this idea of agnosia will be unfolded a lot more as we go, throughout the book. Primarily, agnosia is about being open to adventure and not front-loading it with meaning or expectation but instead going into the unknown with courage—that is to say, without (the need for) knowing what everything means. The greatest adventures are mysterious. We have this urge to know, but it's actually beneficial for us if we don't have the plot spoiler now.

Enjoy the ride. Enjoy your journey.

In the simplicity of our daily lives, this idea means several things to me:

I am not a cockalorum. I don't know everything. In fact, I know very little. I am Dad in our unit, but that does not mean I know everything. I don't even want to know everything. More than that, I don't want to pretend I do. It is a wonderful, exciting thing to embrace the mystery.

I want to yearn in the same way that they do: for discovery, for learning. I want to get excited about an idea or a concept that I don't know anything about. When they become excited about something, I do too. Their curiosity fuels mine.

Deeper than this, I believe that there is a world of knowledge available to us that is beyond rational. It's not materialistic. I believe this is where we get to places of understanding around consciousness, enlightenment, and ultimate discoveries about God and existence. We only have five senses with which to experience this world. Imagine all that exists that we cannot know fully. The butterfly can see hundreds of colors that we cannot.

To exist in the great cloud of unknowing is a powerful and undervalued place to be. Our society pushes us away from this. We are told that we must know. And if you don't know, find out. What if we were to simply enjoy standing in that place of agnosticism, at the cliff of discovery, not in the false comfort of perceived comprehension?

Make Collections
Collections keep you engaged with the world.

Collections are an easy vehicle to make inspired moments happen.

I was taught this notion many years ago and live by it.

If you collect things—rocks, leaves, critters, or (like me) music, ideas, concepts, words, and moments—you have these easy magic lenses with which to explore the world at all times. Because if you're constantly looking for that next perfect leaf, heart-shaped rock, or song that becomes that day's anthem, then everything becomes a treasure. Everything searched for then takes on meaning.

The idea of collecting things is the idea of keeping you in motion, moving forward, and being open to experiencing the world in your own, idiosyncratic way, driven by your own internal reasons.

How to Change and Edit

In our staunch and naked individualism, we are taught to pick a side, have an opinion, and stick to it. And if you change your position on something you're said to be a waffler—unstable, unsure, or wishy-washy.

This, to me, is nonsense.

The world is mutable, and so are we.

We should teach our children that they can change their minds, that they can change their position, and that they should. That is the very definition of learning, growing, and being open to the world and those around them.

And we should help them learn how to do that—especially in the face of differing and challenging opinions—with integrity, courage, vulnerability and an internal confidence and compass. This is how we can inspire others around us to do the same.

This idea is best encapsulated by one of the greatest retorts ever:

> *"When the facts change, I change my mind—*
> *what do you do, sir?"*
> — Popularly attributed to John Maynard Keynes

Sometimes our old maps and stories and myths, although having been of service to us for some time, lose their value. Times change. Our disposition changes. Our attitudes and beliefs shift.

You can feel what's honest to you by concentrating on your

body and how it makes you feel. You can feel what's right more than knowing it sometimes, and this is the perfect place to experiment with that.

Try this experiment: when you say something, try to sink into your body. If you're repeating some old story that you've repeated a hundred times but know that it may not be true for you anymore, you can feel it in your body. That's when it's time to assess this old map and maybe find the courage to either burn it, adapt to it, or edit it.

Play

For us, the notion of play is about remaining excited and engaged with the world around us.

Even on a car ride to the boring store, it's about finding something new—a new song, a new sighting along the road, a new path that we will go back and walk some other time, or a little shack that we haven't seen before buried in the trees.

The idea of play is to say: Tread lightly. Bound. Bounce. Bubble up joyously. Keep looking forward. Keep your head on a swivel.

Being around children, I've had to loosen up, be goofy, and use silly voices. I've improvised when I was feeling sad or moody and joked around when one of the kids was having a hard moment. Sometimes I've even (eek) danced.

Realizing that the world is a playground and that we're actors in our play at all times—able to shift costumes and attitudes and accents and positions—opens up the world to a fun land full of light and endless possibilities.

If you need help getting to this space, just watch your children *play*.

Zone of Proximal Development

The Zone of Proximal Development [ZPD], *created by Lev Vygotsky, is defined as "the space between what a learner can do without assistance and what a learner can do with adult guidance or in collaboration with more capable peers."*[10]

Another way to explain Vygotsky's concept of ZPD is to say that growth only happens in that place where chaos meets order.

Practically it occurs in the kinds of tasks and challenges you place in front of your child. It also happens in the way that you speak to them: you don't speak to them like a baby, but you should speak to them just a bit above where their intellectual skills currently are—as though you're tugging them along into higher and higher dynamics of thought and speech.

This is moving from a beginning point to a new, unnamed point.

In layman's terms, we call this going into the unknown.

---

10 Elsa Billings and Aída Walqui, "Zone of Proximal Development: An Affirmative Perspective in Teaching ELLs," WestEd, accessed May 17, 2022, https://www.wested.org/resources/zone-of-proximal-development/.

The point is not to *lessen fear*, but to *become more courageous*.

The point is to grow alongside your children in tandem, together.

Path and Process

Believe in your path, especially when the night is darkest.

This may be one of the greatest skills I've learned as an adult.

And when the night is so dark you can't read these words in your own mind, then remember:

Amor fati.

Love your fate.

Love where you're at. You're exactly where you need to be for some reason. As uncomfortable as it is, this is where you're at. Find meaning in it—if not now, later.

Pay Attention

We are meaning-making machines. We are story-making machines.

It may just be one of the oldest fundamental truths: Our lives are directly aligned with our motivation for meaning. How we've gone about searching for meaning, what meaning we've gone after, and how well we've succeeded on our soul quests for meaning is mirrored in how we live and who we are.

Stories help link meaning together. We could not survive without the notion of narrative.

The search for meaning and stories is instinctual.

It may even be spiritual.

Conceptually it's the antidote to suffering in all ways. It gives us purpose. Moreover, it may help us clarify existence and the notion of being on our own path. Looking at life this way gives us the indication that there are only patterns and processes. Nothing is stagnant.

When you go about deconstructing a moment, an object, a

word, or a phrase, it's the same as when you create a goal: You become an artist, a builder, your base primal self. You begin ordering chaos. In a cosmic collision inside your head, you begin aligning stars and planets and orienting their spin and stepping back every now and then to see if it makes sense.

Sometimes meaning and story are that abstract. Sometimes meaning is like a painting. It's an aesthetic.

Sometimes meaning and story are concrete and become part of your foundation, part of your space-time fabric.

Pay attention.

Be aware.

Notice the details. Spot the nuances. Find the beauty.

Make meaning and create stories to link meaning together, despite or because of the absurdity of it all.

CHAPTER FOUR

THE MALLEABILITY OF ADVENTURE

Parenting is the ultimate self-transformation tool. I should know—I spent the first year after our separation and subsequent divorce immersed in transformational paradigms instead of going to traditional therapy. And the difference? Everything changed.

In truth, it probably led me to this idea of creative adventuring.

The first time that I picked up the key that was laying on the figurative floor and inserted it into that lock, the door opened effortlessly. It was a "eureka!" moment when all my self-transformation and self-inquiry work in agnosia, post-rationale epistemology, and the theory of no-self began to coalesce in daily practice, when it became yoked to my life as a single parent.

The grand lesson? Whatever you think you should do, examine the opposite first. Your answer is likely embedded there, in the counterintuitive.

"Be water."

—Bruce Lee[11]

---

11 Terry Lee McBride, "Bruce Lee Be as Water My Friend," YouTube, August 14, 2013, video, 0:39, https://www.youtube.com/watch?v=cJMwBwFj5nQ.

Be curious but not too serious.

Go with the flow, and you'll find all you need to know.

You can conceptualize these mottos all you want, but putting them into play is not easy—especially when you know that you have the entire day free tomorrow, so you spend time laboring over a potential itinerary, but you just can't land on something exciting.

After I had come up with this idea of creative adventuring that first pandemic summer, we were energized. We went on adventure after adventure. Mostly, because it was summer, we were in the water: in creeks, lakes, ponds, or rivers.

One night, however, I was determined to put together a different, fresh itinerary.

I was planning on taking us to the U.S. Air Force Academy. It's only 30 minutes away from our new home, the boys love planes, and I wanted them to be impressed by the grand chapel there. But I didn't do my research, and when we got to the gate, the guard informed me that they weren't letting visitors in. COVID struck again.

The lesson here is that sometimes an adventure requires homework. It doesn't always just *happen*.

Lesson relearned.

It's Not a Backup Plan—It's a Moving-Forward Motion

I'd had an idea that I'd need a couple of options for our day, but the second option was an hour and a half away. That's three hours in the car for the babies.

But it was our only good choice.

It's called the Paint Mines. I'd seen photos of it but had never been. It's way out in the grasslands, on the plains—way out.

But once the guard at the Air Force Academy told me we

weren't going to be able to enter the base, I immediately accepted our fate and said, "Gang, we're going on a drive to the surreal grasslands of eastern Colorado." I love driving out there. I always feel as if I'm driving at the bottom of the ocean.

On the Road Again

I knew it was a long drive, possibly a boring one. But I try to make our drives fun.

We listen to children's books on tapes and some kids' podcasts. We stop for snacks and lunch and treats.

We listen to music in the car: *loud*. We sing the songs they love. They ask me to play my favorites. Because of this, I'm constantly needing new music to share with them. We've listened to some songs over a hundred times.

On the road, we talk about everything that you would with six-, four-, and two-year-olds. Frankly, I talk with them more than I talk with anybody else in my life.

We play games, like try to find a red barn, make up a new joke, spot the pretty horses, find a cool car, see the neat building, and where's the next plane, motorcycle, excavator, backhoe, or train.

Then, east of the last town we drove through, there were Cessnas, everywhere—in the sky, on the ground. It was the Calhan Airport. I didn't even know it existed.

As we turned onto the long country road to the east, we passed right by the airfield. The sign said Lessons Available. I said, "We're going to stop there on our way back."

Another 10 miles out, we could see that we were approaching a wind turbine farm. They were lined up on the horizon like gargantuan robots. It was surreal. The whole landscape was surreal.

My very adroit daughter confirmed my nebulous feelings: "Dad, it feels like we're in the ocean."

With the great blue skies above us and the plains spread out in all directions around us, it did feel that way. It always has.

I said, "You know, as we learned at the dinosaur museum, this actually was an ocean. If we were here about 200 million years ago, we would have been driving on the seafloor."

About 230 million years ago, it rained for a million years on planet Earth. And Colorado was buried under a warm, shallow sea called the Western Interior Seaway.

The Paint Mines

We stopped at the wind turbine farm. There were maybe a hundred or so of them. They make eerie sounds. I couldn't imagine living by them on a silent night. So creepy.

(These turbines are actually a nightmare for the residents, causing them a lot of health problems and aesthetic unpleasantries.)

In the middle of the turbine farm, oddly, were the mines.

The Paint Mines are a badland kind of place. It's a field of weathered, striated, and colored steeples, pinnacles, curtains, gullies, and hoodoos, or eroded spires with mushroom-like caps. The sandstone formations are all kinds of colors. The ground and the gullies are covered in white sand or dust.

It was over 90 degrees that day, and there was no shade cover, so I knew our time was limited. So, we motored. Down the steep incline, we went down and into the mines. We explored all the gullies we could, culminating with the "discovery" of a great *Goonies* cave that provided some respite from the blazing sun (pictured left).

The mines are gorgeous and weird looking. The kids loved exploring all the nooks and crannies and getting dirty.

With red-beaten cheeks, we hustled back up and onto the wide-open grasslands after we found the cave.

I disrobed each of them since their clothes were all white with that dusty chalk of the sandstone. I wiped them down, changed a poopy diaper, then gave them water and a Lunchable. Completely wiped out, we drove back into Calhan.

Strawberry Milk

We stopped at the airfield and watched a couple of Cessnas take off and land. My four-year-old kept remarking about how he wanted to "learn how to drive one of those planes." And so I excitedly began to build a lesson plan around that for him.

I believe in praise. I believe in motivating by encouragement. It's my management style.

It always has been, and I'm not shirking away from it now. In fact, I'm leaning deeper into it.

Because they were so brave and did so great helping each other through the Paint Mines, and they stuck together as a family and unit, I told them I'd buy them a treat.

We settled on strawberry milk.

And so, we drove back to Denver with pink mustaches while we listened to *Where the Wild Things Are* and other books on tape as my youngest dozed off.

So where one plan fell through, another sprouted and then surprised us with a multitude of gorgeous, surreal experiences.

Wind and water made those sandstone mines. Wind and water are about movement and softness. Once again, I was reaffirmed in my notion that rigidity born from disappointment is not the answer. The answer, the response to anything should be "Be water."

Be water.

CHAPTER FIVE

LOVE WITHOUT OWNERSHIP

Loving romantically without ownership is one thing.

Try loving your children without feeling ownership over them. That is hard.

But divorce will certainly teach you that.

(Maybe everything from now on should just be called "What I Learned Through Divorce")

Romantic love has roots in commerce and ownership, so it's no wonder that we head in that direction from the beginning. But it's the language that calcifies it:

My girl. My man. Mine.

Everything in our culture around marriage and the like sounds like a selfish child: taking.

But with children, with *my* children ... that's different.

Right?

Saying Goodbye

Early on, it was difficult for me.

When we were married and when one of our babies would go stay at their grandparents for the night or for a weekend, I would have a very difficult time. Even when I've left them to go to work, I've sometimes struggled.

Sure, I've acknowledged that I'm a bit different from others. At the time, my ex-wife seemed lighter when they would leave. And sure, even I felt the respite and indulged in the possibilities: I'd get to sleep in later. The house would be quiet. I could catch up on chores: laundry, cleaning, etc.

But I'd always eagerly await their return. On one such return, we put up streamers on the front porch as a kind of celebration. The oldest two were little babies at that point; their youngest brother wasn't even a concept then. But when their grandparents pulled up in their vehicle, the kids were not impressed, nor did they understand why it was such a big deal for them to come back home.

But it was a big deal for me, because they were mine. This was the life I'd ordained in that fashion: *they were mine*. I wanted them so badly that I am still, to this day, lovesick even when I am with them.

All that said is quite interesting. I never wanted to have children. But then it all changed the first time my ex-wife said, "I'm pregnant." A gear clicked. Every molecule in my body flipped. Ever since then, the strongest impulse in my life at all times is to be with my kids.

But now, because of divorce, once a week, my babies leave me.

And it is devastating. Confusing.

For three nights in a row, I was without them in the beginning. And that seemed like an eternity. Now, I'm without them for five days at a time, and that is … disorienting.

For somebody who struggled with his children leaving just for the weekend, or even a night, this has proven to be monumental and heartbreaking, sometimes destructively so.

In quiet, I will talk to myself about how I now live a compromised life, a life full of goodbyes and a life of constant transition. I now live a life that's like always coming back from vacation, when I'm dreading the comedown back to reality.

And I do dread the goodbyes. Even when I'm with them, I live with pangs of sadness, because they inevitably must leave again.

So, I have told myself, I have two choices: I can live with this paralyzing sadness, which feels as if it's bordering on pity. Or I can do something about it.

Again, I've leaned into self-inquiry work as a workaround to discover "hacks" and, ultimately, a new paradigm.

I've decided on living in motion in high resolution—no more low-resolution half-guesses.

This new way of life and my acceptance of it have created so much grief in me; in my body, there's unnameable constriction. In my mind, there are labyrinths. But the thing is, this old fear and grief doesn't even belong to me. When I think about this blockage, this constriction that articulates itself physically as a hot anvil behind my sternum, I can even see it: it's rigid. It's calcified. And it's not mine.

I do believe that, just like information, grief is passed down from those before us, from our ancestors through the generations. And, if not that, then I certainly believe that the coping mechanisms we're taught are passed down.

Grief is information.

Healing that grief puts us in formation.

Romantic Love as Rooted in Parenting

You know all those love songs all around us? Well, I contend that all of them ever written, if you extract the mature and sexual elements from the songs, were written about my love for my children.

If I'm not careful, this won't come out correctly, but it's true. When we're in the car or even in a store—anywhere—I'll be singing along or just listening to the lyrics in those songs, and what strikes me is one thing: Man, this is pretty much how I feel about my children—love and longing and the beauty of existence and the fear of loving something that death can take away.

I strongly believe that our notion of soul mates came from parenting. It came from the knowledge of the parents' love of their child. I believe that all of our views on marriage and romantic love in the postmodern age come from our ancient history and relationship with parenting. We wanted to mirror that profundity—the highest of all virtues encapsulated—in a romantic love partner. We wanted to find salvation in that love, hope in that connection, and safety in that dangerous thing we call love.

But alas, parental love and romantic love and the art we've created around capital *L* Love is all built from entirely disparate foundations and modes of operation: our notions of romantic love are not sustainable. They're not even real. They're a fantasy.

Research has told us that the idea of romantic love and marriage is a newer concept, accepted and concretized in only about the 18th century.[12] For thousands of years, the idea of mixing romantic love and marriage was considered a dangerous idea. As for our contemporary idea of marriage—the ideas of courtly love from southern France—even the French thought that this kind of romantic love did not belong in marriage.[13]

Marriage has existed for about 4,400 years, but in the last 40

---

12   Katie Barclay and Sally Holloway, "Interrogating Romantic Love," *The Journal of the Social History Society* 17, no. 3 (2020): 271–277, https://doi.org/10.1080/14780038.201 9.1685839.

13   *Stephanie Coontz: On Marriage. YouTube*, 2011. https://www.youtube.com/ watch?v=gwtb7jz8G4k.

years, it has changed dramatically.[14] And it has skewed our notions of love. A call for a new and sustainable way to define love is necessary.

Soul mates and that kind of attempt at love are all about attachment. It *is*, in fact, dangerous. It's needy, volatile. It is, again, a fantasy. It undercuts the autonomy of the beloved as an object to be subdued and owned.

What is real? The love a parent has for their child.

You know, when I was in my twenties and I heard about people only aspiring to be a parent, I thought it was a lousy, weak way to go. And I partially still believe that—if that's all you have. But just to be a parent: yes, I have learned that it is probably the greatest gift we are given and the greatest gift we can give. If not that, then it sure feels that way. It sure feels more profound than any other emotion or connection or drive that I have in my body and mind.

Love as Nonattachment

Through my self-inquiry work, I've realized that love is counterintuitive. It doesn't work the way I thought it did, the way I was taught.

Love requires *letting go*.

And no, not in that cliché way that you always hear about in the movies.

Through self-inquiry work, self-transformation work, or even enlightenment work as it's sometimes called, I've undertaken myriad meditations and been privy to countless fresh paradigms that are actually ages old. These are some of the oldest ideas known to man.

What I've concluded is that I can do two things: hang on and squeeze the kids to death, or let go.

---

14 "The Origins of Marriage," *The Week,* January 8, 2015, https://theweek.com/articles/528746/origins-marriage.

And what I know, through the practices I've learned and implemented—some out of near-desperation for sanity—is that letting go is the best solution.

Letting go makes the most sense.

Once you start doing it and you get over the lumpy beginning where it feels awkward and bulbous and wrong, it metamorphoses. It starts to work.

It works.

> *"Hands are unbearably beautiful. They hold on to things.*
> *They let things go."*
> — Mary Ruefle[15]

Sometimes the Hardest Thing Is the Right Thing

Love is counterintuitive.

At least, it's more counterintuitive from the ways I was taught, from what the movies showed me, and from what the love songs told me.

Looking at love as an act of nonattachment now doesn't seem so strange. But, at first, it really, truly was. I'm almost embarrassed by how difficult it has been to wriggle out of that mindset.

I oscillate between succeeding and then falling back into old habits, wherein clutching on to what you thought you rightfully owned was the only thing that made sense and the way things have always worked. That's what a man does, right? He takes ownership.

It's as the inquiry work has told me and then shown me: Your ego isn't going to like this. Your ego wants to latch on. Your ego doesn't want to let go. Your ego is telling you, "It's yours, take it. Don't let anybody else have it."

As I learned from the inquiry work even before some of the med-

---

15   Mary Ruefle, "The Cart" in *Selected Poems* (Seattle: Wave Books, 2010), 51.

itations, this is not going to feel good. You may even feel sick moving through this liminality. Why? Because your ego wants what it wants, and it thinks it's protecting itself by acting as it does.

But the fact of the matter is, most of the time, your ego is acting in a way that may temporarily satiate a need or desire, but for the long term, it will create toxicity.

The way I now conceptualize my ego is that it's a robot interested in one thing: self-preservation. It creates mechanisms so that it won't walk itself off a cliff or injure itself. If I really dig into this idea, I can even experience this selfish ego. I can feel it in my body, namely behind my sternum—where fear lives.

I can often stop these thoughts to the point that I can ultimately recognize this attempt at self-preservation as violence. Sometimes it's so overwhelming that I get vertigo.

One meditation (and no, don't think of meditation in the yogic, sitting-on-the-mat-for-hours sense) that I can dive into is around stories: "It's my ego that is the thing that keeps me from walking off cliffs." It's actually my ego that says, "You should go to the doctor to get that checked out."

Our egos keep us safe, not necessarily happy. Our egos intend on protecting us. But that protection comes at a cost. And what our egos' intents are is not always what we want.

My ego does not want to be destroyed even more than I don't want to be destroyed.

This is where my life has led me: everything, e v e r y t h i n g, pivots on destroying this thing that I've identified with for over 40 years.

In the first place, to fully love myself, I know that I have to let go.

Of my ego.

Of hanging on.

To fully love my children, I know that I have to do the same thing: let go.

Love as Transition

Love is counterintuitive.

As life goes, so does love. Because love is composed of myriads of virtues, it's about transitions.

In the least, it's about transitioning from one emotion to the next.

At least, this is what divorce has taught me, even though I knew it from years of research: when an emotion comes, grab it, observe it, but then when the time comes, let it go.

As I've gone through the heavy transitions I've had in my life, I've put this into practice.

I don't think that you can truly understand the gravity of the lessons you need to until you are conscious of them and then are able to practice them under chaotic duress.

Sure, I've gone through periods of transition, periods of incredibly heavy emotion. These were about me moving from one place in my life to the next, and often, they hurt so much they caused months-long disorientation.

One reason was I was never good at letting go. I didn't understand the notion of transitioning. I didn't understand that there are no "things," only processes. I didn't know that everything is always in flux.

Now, I have one simple tool, among others, that enables me to be more fluid, to move: *let go*. When an unwanted thought about something comes, I have a practice: let it go. Sometimes, on a bad day, I do this over 50 times.

But it's paying off.

The Children

This is going to sound goofy, but I'm going to say it aloud for the first time: the children don't belong to me, they belong to the universe or nothing.

My despair over not being able to see them for half of their lives is selfish. And I'm not meeting the situation with radical acceptance. They love their mom, they need her, and they want her.

This has been one of the most difficult things to, well, hold on to.

I have to let go of them in a way that a traditional, nuclear family would not have to.

But for this, I am better. I am a better parent.

Because of this, I love them harder when I'm with them.

Because of this, I try to help them capitalize on all our moments together.

Because of this, I help them overcome attachment with their emotions.

Because I am a model for them.

I have to model and embody this behavior, because I want this more than I want my ego.

And what I know is that letting go is the best thing to do, for them and myself.

And I would have never discovered this central paradigm if it weren't for our nightmare of a divorce.

Still, don't be fooled: It's brutal when they leave. The house goes from chaos to silence. It feels as if the pale of death has lowered itself down. And in a way, it has. It feels like grief whenever they leave. And while it's often torturous for me, and I spend deliberate time grieving and sobbing, there is a blessing in it.

Let go. *Let go.*

How Do You Know?

I know that letting go is the right thing to do because I know that attachment creates pain inside me. And that pain leads to dis-ease, and then disease.

Once I made the transition from thinking to feeling my body, it was obvious. For example, I can, right now, feel where fear resides in my body. I know where it hides and lives if I let it.

And now, because I've put in the practice, I know how to move fear or any unwanted emotion through my body and let it pass organically.

I know that letting go is the right thing to do because when I grip onto my children, I create pain inside of them. It's not visible or immediately perceptible pain, but it's the pain of emotional unintelligence. It's the pain of neediness.

These are the kinds of wounds that you create inside a child, and as invisible as these wounds are, they are even more insidious. The wounds may not present themselves for many years in explicit ways, but once they do, they can do so in very covert, often seemingly irreversible ways.

I've learned this lesson through our creative adventuring. When you are rigid over the outcome that you want, you can destroy a whole day.

Even when I'm determined to get my daughter to sit down and do homework, and she is resisting it to the point that no work is getting done—despite the fact it must get done and even though my schedule needs it to happen now—often, shifting gears and moving them into a different space for a while and then shifting her back into homework mode enables me to get her back to a place where she can truly get that work done.

The more you hold on, the tighter you grip on to the idea you want to happen, the more resistance it creates.

How do you let go of something? You don't do it with the same force applied to gripping the object or item. You simply let go.

Clench your fist tightly. When you decide to undo that fist, how do you do it? Not with the same force you applied in holding the fist together. To undo that fist, you apply the opposite amount of pressure. Zero pressure. You let go.

Counterintuitive, see?

> *"To understand life is to let yourself be carried away like a cork in a river."*
>
> — Renoir (2012)[16]

---

16 *Renoir*, directed by Gilles Bourdos (2012; France: Mars Distribution).

CHAPTER SIX

WHAT'S IN OUR ADVENTURE BAG?

I learned a valuable lesson early on that changed all our adventuring for the better: I forgot bug repellent. I just forgot to pack it in the sack.

We went down to our creek one late spring evening. Yes, in the evening when all the mosquitos come out to feast.

I was devastated: My daughter's face was destroyed—giant bites all over the most beautiful face on this planet. I was ashamed.

But instead of going too far with my ineptitude, I chose to take it as a blessing. It taught me the value of thinking clearly and calmly and double- or triple-checking our pack before leaving. And upon returning from adventures and trips, I clean the bag, restock it, and evaluate it.

If there is one theme in creative adventuring, it is that every folly becomes a teaching moment.

What I noticed upon reflection was: In the chaos of gearing up and getting everybody ready, I simply left the repellent on the credenza when I had pulled everything out of the bag to repack.

Sure, I've forgotten their water bottles before. That was an easy remedy: We just stopped and bought disposable bottles. It's hard to remember everything. But with the repellent, I didn't know we needed it until we were knee-deep in the muddy creek bottom, with no turning back.

The lesson embedded here is to *slow down.* It's only my responsibility to make sure they're comfortable and protected and safe.

So now, after we return home and I pull out all the sandy, dirty clothes and dirty dishes, I clear out the rest of the detritus (usually rocks and sticks they want me to keep), and I put the essentials back in first (repellent, sunscreen, first aid kit). I leave visual cues about what I need to do in the morning to repack the sack.

Again, my kiddos are six, four, and two, so what we carry in our pack is probably different from what others carry.

What Do We Carry in Our Daypack?
- Bug repellent (We used to only use organic spray, but in Colorado, we need the repellent with DEET for mosquitos and ticks.)
- Sunscreen
- Water bottles, full (I carry a Camelback hydration water pack as well.)
- First aid kit
- Medicine, including ibuprofen, acetaminophen, and Pepto-Bismol
- Knife
- Nail clippers
- Diapers
- Water Wipes
- One change of clothes for each kid
- Water bottles
- Snacks and lunch

We are only out for, max, four to six hours, so a small 25-liter pack is sufficient. We do have larger packs for the bigger outings we have planned. And the kids have responsibilities for transporting gear too. I typically find that they want to be part of the process and like the structure and the responsibility in the same way that they like to be the leader of our expedition.

I always keep the following supplies in the car:

- A beach tent (It's genius; setting up and striking it takes just a minute.)
- Packable picnic blankets
- Fleece blankets
- Towels
- Water and sprayer for cleaning up
- Plenty of hats, from trucker style to packable sombrero sun hats
- Plenty of jackets, mostly fleece, and sweatshirts
- My muck boots (highly recommended for creek tromping)
- Propane stove and pot
- First aid kit
- Inflatable pump (for floats and mattresses)
- Oars for our boat

CHAPTER SEVEN

CREEKING

I t's called "creeking."

It's probably our favorite thing to do.

It's free.

There's usually nobody else around where we go.

And what this activity reinforces is the idea that you don't need expensive toys to entertain children. You really don't even need money. You just need a creek—some rocks, sticks, and water. Whatever living critters you run into are a bonus. Lately, my four-year-old just wants to make mud castles everywhere we go.

Creeking teaches us all about so much: leadership, coordination, decision-making, flora, fauna, risk and danger, and, yes, adventure.

I can remember the firsts.

I remember the first time they heard a bullfrog.

I remember the first time they spotted a raptor's nest; the first time they became obsessed with collecting all the Asian clamshells that had washed ashore from the reservoir; and their first time standing on a beaver dam, talking them through the mechanics and reasoning of it all, showing them the trees gnawed down, and spotting the beaver in the water.

We've learned about toads and how they're mildly poisonous

and scalier and slower than frogs. We've learned about tadpoles, fish fries, the great white herons, and the geese when they come in from the creeks to the lakes at dusk to reclaim their great wide open.

But we've also learned how to be together—teamwork—and most importantly, *how to push through adversity*.

Sometimes it's not easy. Bushwhacking can take a toll. The kids' legs can get cut up. They get tired. There are bugs, mosquitos, and ticks. It gets dirty and muddy and sweaty, or sometimes, a little cold.

And sometimes, because we're sauntering without complete aim and we're often somewhere I've never traveled, we get lost. We wade through marshes and wetlands. Dad has had them slop it through the up-to-the-knees mud in dense, emergent undergrowth, then push through the cattails and oak and cottonwood until we heard or saw the stream.

"Because it's over there … somewhere. We're getting close."

"Dad …"

"I think this is a bad idea …"

I cheered them on: "C'mon guys. It'll be worth it."

"You can do it."

"C'mon, gang!"

Then: *voilà!* We emerged into an open alluvial plain and our stream. So gorgeous the light was. The small falls and bends splashed while the aspens quaked in the evening light. The yarrow and the bulrush glistened, waving back and forth, welcoming us to this secret place. The sound of water was everywhere. Life became watery and suddenly easy. Even the grasses and trees contributed to the symphony of watery sound and overwhelmed our ears.

Then, the kids' demeanors, their attitudes, *transformed*.

Suddenly, I couldn't keep them near me. They bounded off,

skipping like stones over the water, from one sandbank to another.

There were offshoots of the creek, eddies and new, unexplored, untouched routes back into the tangle of the marshland of cattails and wooded things. There were waterfalls and deadfalls, obstacles, and opportunities for wonder, for magic, for whole new secret worlds.

"Dad! This place is amazing!"

Dad was right. *Whew.*

Failure was so, so close.

Fortune was on our side, yet again.

It was a new creek. There was no path to it, and there were three babies in the brush taller than they were. I led the bushwhacking through and over and under, with knee-deep mud all over us, until we knelt down in the cool creek, with the sunset streaming in on a warm sandbank, and I cleaned the kids up, one at a time.

My two-year-old (who was one at the time) was so excited about this new place and his ability to spring onto the soft, sprawling sandbanks. He tripped over his own feet and smashed into the water enough that, with the sunlight waning and the heat of the day drifting away, I had to change him immediately as he shivered with glee in front of me.

Pack Your Bags

I cleaned the babies up, put on dry shorts, changed shirts, and wiped their faces—back to normal.

One of my favorite sensations is when one of the kids needs something, and I have it. A dry shirt. Neosporin. A Band-Aid. A diaper. More bug spray. Water. Snacks. A hat.

Whew. I had what we needed.

There's something magical about standing on a bank in late spring, with the orange light on the swishing and swashing buckwheat and foxtail. The colors of everything were so rich, and all our senses were awake and poignant and bright. That magic extended to re-dressing my one-year-old who was so cold that his lips were blue, but his blue eyes were bigger than mine, and they weren't cold; they were scanning the creek for the next thing he was going to go explore as soon as his concerned dad got him redressed in a dry shirt and shorts.

I inhaled all of it as if I was inhaling all the flowers in the land, but I was really just inhaling pure relief in a breezy evening. The sounds of my six- and four-year-olds came from just out of my sightline—but I could still hear them, so I knew they were OK.

Then my one-year-old stepped into an eddy and soaked his shorts—again. He looked back at me. He was shivering.

My stomach turned once before I remembered that I had packed a second pair of shorts that either of the boys could wear. They fit them both. Again, I inhaled with relief.

We keep our outfitting fairly basic because we're only gone for a couple of hours at a time. That and I'm typically carrying my two-year-old on my shoulders, so I don't want the pack to weigh me down any more than necessary.

Good water shoes are the most important element: no sandals or flip-flops. You need shoes with traction for slick rocks and moss and mud, but you also need shoes that are going to stay on.

I prefer for the kids to wear swimsuits. I'll strip them down when we get to the car in some manner as they're always muddy and sandy. I keep a weed sprayer in the back of the car with water in it to clean them up. Mud and sand are tricky beasts to wipe away.

If temperatures drop into the 60s and 50s, I'll make sure to have the kids' fleece jackets packed and a small towel to wipe faces and feet. Blankets are in the car for our ride back home, since the kids will be tired and spent, overloaded by the sensory bath we took out in the wild.

The Effort Is the Payoff

Creeking is one example of an adventure that requires a lot of work—especially when it's three versus one.

But the reward is just too great to ignore.

If you pack well and prepare and learn from your mistakes, it becomes easier.

It costs no money. And while you do need to pay attention to who owns the water rights on some areas of the creeks, the watery highway is a safe place to open the envelope to a very simple sense of adventure.

I find it intriguing that the word "creeking" has an alternative definition from the Urban Dictionary:

"To creek: to overthink a situation or feeling until it is far more complicated than it really is. Taken from the teen drama of the

'90s *Dawson's Creek*, where teenagers would overthink/have far more than necessary deep and meaningful conversations."[17]

It's interesting because creeking taught me the interplay between preparing well and thinking soundly about your adventure ahead. But when you don't know where you're exactly going and just go instead, you have to turn off your brain a little in order to wander into some kind of inspired, ecstatic place of discovery.

There's effort in preparing for an adventure.

There's also effort in letting go and just going.

---

17 Urban Dictionary, s.v. "creeking (*v.*)," April 22, 2009, https://www.urbandictionary.com/define.php?term=Creeking.

CHAPTER EIGHT

SAUNTERING

Saunter. Go on a desultory stroll. All this is to say, go but have no aim—just go with no rigid purpose into the unknown.

Of course, you can't completely do that blindly with three babies. So, in this spirit, have *some* purpose, just not a lot. I mean, you need to mark your map. Know where you are, roughly. Know how far you are from help. Know your resources and your limits.

But, sometimes, if you just simply *go*, the world will start revealing itself to you.

What is sauntering? To walk with a leisurely gait.

Thoreau expounded on this notion wonderfully:

> I have met with but one or two persons in the course of my life who understood the art of walking, that is, of taking walks—who had a genius, so to speak, for sauntering, which word is beautifully derived "from idle people who roved about the country, in the Middle Ages, and asked charity, under pretense of going a la Sainte Terre, to the Holy Land, till the children exclaimed, "There goes a Sainte-Terrer," a Saunterer, a Holy-Lander. Some, however, would derive the word from sans terre, without land or a home, which, there-

fore, in the good sense, will mean, having no particular home, but equally at home everywhere. For this is the secret of successful sauntering.[18]

Another articulation of this is with the notion of a desultory stroll. This is a stroll without aim or method, a kind of swerving.

Core Values

Sauntering anchors us back into our core beliefs of creative adventuring:

- Evoke curiosity by asking questions.
  Where are we going? Why are we here?
- Agnosia
  The idea of "I don't know" is sometimes the best answer and an excellent place to start the turbine of curiosity.
- Seek out novel situations.
  What is here, where are we going, and why?
- Selflessness
  When you just go, you lose the need to know. For me as the parent, I lose all sense of myself in some large regard because, when we're exploring and don't know the end game, my focus is on the kiddos and their location, safety, and comfort.
- Adversity
  To walk into the unknown requires courage and trust.
- Appreciate subtle novelty.
  See new, little moments and clues and things that make this certain place magical.
- Open experience and gaps—don't close them.
  Be open to the adventure without trying to fit it in a pre-

---

18 Henry David Thoreau, "Walking," *The Atlantic,* May 1862, https://www.theatlantic.com/magazine/archive/1862/06/walking/304674/.

conceived box of what it's supposed to be.

- Collections

  What is here that we can add to our collections? Can we start a new collection because of this place?

- Believe in your path

  Even when you're just creating your path in the wild, believe.

- Be able to change and edit and be wrong.

  Dad picked a bad trail. The stream has no water in it. Sometimes what I think is going to bore them gives them hours of endless fun, and new discoveries abound.

Make Magic Happen

So, we have a basic outline for a plan. Have goals: we're driving to this lake, heading down to that bridge, going over to that sandbar, walking to that beach ...

We go sauntering. In our car. On foot. On our scooters. Our bikes. Sometimes, via all four modes of transport.

Magical morsels will appear, like a new, undiscovered place that you didn't know about—even though it was right around the corner. An abandoned shed in the forest. A tipi. A gem shop. A pickle store. An airfield. A wind turbine farm. The North Pole that we encountered driving up Pikes Peak. The gift shop with great donuts at the top of that peak.

But it's even simpler than this: find a hill, a meadow, a pond, a creek, or any other geologic surprises you may encounter around you.

Whatever you discover, it's even more simple than that. We find great sticks. We find bones.

It's as simple as your six-year-old looking up and saying, "Dad, I think that's a raptor's nest." Sure enough, she was right. So, we kept our eyes on it, waiting to see the giant shadow of wings or an aerial chase circling above us.

And one day, sure enough, when we were there, under the nest but not even thinking about it, there she was: a big red-tailed hawk gliding above us, scanning the fields, looking for supper before the thunderous storm coming in from the north landed.

Magic. It happens if you put yourself in a place where it can.

CHAPTER NINE

STAY YOUNG, SON

There's a pressure in raising two boys.

There's the same but very different pressure in raising a girl.

It can be a pressure, or it can become an adventure.

Raising any gender has its hurdles.

One hurdle I've noticed with my boys is the convention and the pressure *to grow up*.

It's a very vocal convention.

Be a big boy.

Grow up.

Be a man.

At 46 years of age, I still feel this pressure.

So, let's talk about how we release this old paradigm, because we need to. It hasn't worked for a long time.

Conventions, Inventions

We are intellectually lazy creatures. We rely on tradition, patterns, mores, and etiquettes. We rely on societal morals, on the dominant paradigms, accepted rituals, and common practices.

When it comes to children, the reliance on convention is almost hyperbolic.

And it's fine to have a median, a touchstone and measuring stick, or an accepted paradigm.

But the thing is, conventions are often wrong. They perhaps served a purpose at one time, but they then become archaic and nonoperational.

If something becomes outdated, it needs to become updated.

But this is the thing about conventions and all we lean on: we lean on them because we're lazy. Then, oops, sometimes we forget to update them, sometimes for a century or two.

We've had an idea in our society that children become adults at eighteen. A hundred years ago, I can see why this needed to be the case.

Now, not so much.

Life expectancy is much higher.

And now science is saying that the prefrontal cortex doesn't fully develop until something like 25, 26, or 27 years old. Research is now saying that boys are not ready to be men and leave late adolescence until almost their 30s.

Their 30s.

The Assimilation

We begin shoving conventions on children at a young age. We try to make them like us. We try to put them in our boxes. Nay, they aren't even our boxes but our ancestors' boxes.

We have it backward.

We should be listening to children, especially infants and toddlers, for insight into what they're modeling, for what's developmentally appropriate for them, and for the moments when new possibilities can be absorbed by them.

I know—it sounds so "new age." Foofy.

What are we missing in the narrative of the good life? Shockingly, some of the answers could be right under our noses, embedded in the creatures that we have dismissed.

We've long had it backward.

Up until recently, we didn't think that we could learn much of anything from the young ones. Clearly, their skill sets haven't evolved. Their intellect and their problem-solving needs some work.

But watch an infant: They let go of things perfectly. They flow with the world. They live in a flow state much more than we do. They're often moving from pure states of joyous discovery. They have no funny social games. If you watch them, they swing from tree to tree in the woods much more elegantly than we attachment-addicted adults do.

We should be *listening* to them instead of *talking* so much at them.

"The purpose of art is washing the dust of daily life off our souls. The chief enemy of creativity is 'good sense.'
It takes a long time to become young."
— Pablo Picasso

The Culprit

Many of the behaviors and traits we've been indoctrinated with in our upbringing have created bondage and limitation in our lives.

The central player in this enslavement is our ego.

In a way, it's not even that we're sometimes trying to place the children in certain cognitive boxes as much as it is that they are trying to fit themselves into those boxes out of necessity to acculturate, to fit in.

As we develop, we devise a complex network of ideas about who we are. These ideas become our egos. They become our identity or our identities, plural. These can help create a structure around us: a sense of common understanding, a meaning. It's necessary for the cognitive development of the child. But as we age, we develop many roles that we play over the course of a single day, and we become fixated and dependent on them.

Think about how many times you have been told, felt the need, or wanted to *be somebody.*

It's our strong attachment to this drive and these identities that creates damage and confusion. Part of the reason this occurs is that these functions pull us away from our authentic identity, our true self, and the natural state we were born into.

What Does the Ego Do That's So Bad?

Since the dawn of thinking, ancient wisdom has always said that the ego is fiction, or that it's trouble. It's the cause of perhaps all pain in our lives. And our addiction to all our illusory, multiple identities is the result of that false story of the ego.

One problem is that the ego is incredibly talky. Stop and listen to it. When you become aware of it, you will be shocked at how much unnecessary talk there is going on inside your head all the time.

There's constant noise *all day long.*

Within this talk comes another downfall: our ego labels everything *obsessively*—dangerously.

This leads to our ego judging everything all the time. Often it misjudges. Often it misperceives or misinterprets. And what happens then?

Answer: *trouble.*

It wasn't always that way.

The Monkey Chatter

Kids can turn off the noise, that monkey chatter, better.

You can see this in their ability to nearly forget things and to let things go so quickly. They succeed more because they don't have so many long-standing, entrenched beliefs and stories that are constantly measuring everything around them.

Newborns and infants and, I'd argue, even toddlers are *directly experiencing*. They are hungry, thirsty, in pain, etc. They are not layering too many thoughts over these direct experiences. As a result, they are not layering *concepts* over their raw experiences. These thoughts, these adult, human-made concepts are never the actual. They are make-believe.

Especially with infants, the ego hasn't developed yet. Infants are undifferentiated masses of being experiencing phenomena. Language hasn't come online. An infant hasn't invented, or learned, distinctions between self, other, and world.

In short, children have less monkey chatter in their brains.

In other words, they're *thinking* less but *doing* more.

They're *being* more.

The cognitive structures that our cultures place around children assimilating and finding their identities are the culprit. We typically call this function: *thinking*. And for millennia we've placed a high value on it. The truth is, it's advanced our society, but at the same time it's stood in the way of a true understanding of our authentic sense of self and the deeper mysteries of our universe and of existence.

Ah, what a paradoxical existence we lead.

Thinking is useful for technological advancements and understanding the outside world. But it's not useful when we explore the inside world or when we think we're obstructing our knowledge of our true self.

Acculturalization for children is the act of becoming ignorant of the self, of becoming distant from the authentic self. Acculturalization and assimilation are the mechanisms that create the chatty Cathy inside all of us.

On the converse, infants and even toddlers are in a natural state of unthinking.

It's we adults who force them to think. And worse, we force them *to think like us*.

The kids aren't juggling all the identities that we are. They aren't addicted to them or bound to them. As a result, children have less internal monologue, less monkey chatter in the brain. They are one step closer to the stillness and silence of pure existence and unadulterated consciousness.

The best way I've learned to be somebody is to *be nobody*.

To be nobody is to be back again in that childlike state, that toddler state, that infant state.

Be a Man, Not a Boy

I hear these things. I've even said some of these things. They've come flying out of my mouth like a bad habit.

And they are not what we should be teaching:

Quit drinking from a bottle.
You're a big boy.
Put on your underwear; you shouldn't be wearing a diaper.
Don't you want to be a big boy?
Quit crying.
Big boys don't cry.

Why is it such an imperative that our boys become big men so quickly? We come out of the womb so helpless.

We should be teaching lessons that accord with each child's time frame, abilities, and proclivities. We shouldn't be trying to shove each kid into the same box, a box built by our ancestors, with maps that we can't even read in the native tongue anymore.

I say, Stay young, son.

You'll be a man soon enough.

When the time is right, and I've helped position you with the resources and guidance you need, you'll be ready.

You'll be ready soon enough. I'll make sure of that. It's my number one job.

Enjoy every boyish delight, for your map about how to live successfully is probably embedded in exactly how you're existing right now. The information is in everything around you and inside you.

And if I listen to this advice, of indulging in your youth, it will help me too. For if I want to live a conscious life of being awake, I should probably be listening to you more, instead of talking at you all the time.

CHAPTER TEN

SASQUATCH

We found Sasquatch.

Kind of.

On our way up to the top of Pikes Peak one day, I spotted a sign (*pictured left*). I went into my mental recall and couldn't remember any stories about Bigfoot in Colorado.

Thirty minutes earlier we were standing inside the North Pole, a tourist trap of a place on the toll road up to Pikes Peak. I thought this Bigfoot sign was maybe just a gimmick.

It's not. Turns out, the area around Pikes Peak is very rich in Bigfoot lore. You can hear about a good number of Colorado sightings on a great resource, the *You Don't Know Squatch* podcast.

We continued upward and summited.

Way up there, 14,115 feet above sea level, there's a gift shop. Inside is a 10-foot-tall Sasquatch. At its feet are Mr. and Mrs. Bigfoot stuffed animals. My son, stunned by the massive beast before him, articulated that he wanted a stuffy, so we got it (pictured with him, left). On our way back down, we found the Bigfoot sign again, and that's when my children's fascination was born. They were hooked before we even talked much about it.

On the ride home, I told them what I knew.

When we got home, my daughter wanted to know more. She wanted to watch things about Bigfoot. I showed her the Patterson-Gimlin film. She was not super impressed. She wanted more. We then found Squatch-hunter shows. She was locked in.

I didn't know we had sightings in Colorado until that day.

A new obsession was born.

The Mystery

I had always been curious about the quest for Sasquatch in the same way that I'm intrigued by the stories of lost treasure, forgotten cities and cultures, arcane places and supernatural sites, UFOs and alien life-forms, the cosmos, God, or the quest for our authentic self.

This is what Sasquatch is for me: it's a symbol. A representation. A metaphor.

Sasquatch is a representation of exploration, adventure, and mystery; it's a quest, or a cabal.

For me, Bigfoot has always been about hidden mysteries and secrets. It's something that happens under the cover of night, out in the woods. It's something you must put effort into finding.

It's said that you can typically smell them before you see them.

It's said that they snap trees way up on the trunk (eight to nine feet) on trails to mark territory.

It's said that they twist tree branches into strange configurations and arches. These could not happen naturally. They're the work of a strong creature with strong hands.

It's said that they throw rocks at people.

The evidence and sightings are fascinating.

Are the claims true or not? I don't know.

I do know that this has been a story that has been pervasive in Western culture for nearly a thousand years. Since the Middle

Ages in Europe, they called it the "Wild Man."[19]

Truth? *I don't really care if there is or isn't an actual Sasquatch.*

What I'm sure about is that *I don't ever want one to actually be found.*

I want the search to go on and on and on, because what's important is the mystery. The adventure. The learning. The editing of ideas. The escalation of wonder. The reverence created for the woods and the creatures in them.

Bigfoot is not an animal.

Bigfoot is an allegory. Embedded in that story are the hidden meanings of how to live life.

There's a Big, Scary World Out There

I know the world really is dangerous and scary.

And I know your kids, my kids, will encounter some of these scary ideas, concepts, and visuals.

I've heard that *Bigfoot is scary to the kids.*

My response? No, it's not, not if you're creatively parenting your children.

Parent them. Flip the script. *Educate them.*

Try this film on them: *The Son of Bigfoot.*[20] My kids are obsessed with this movie. The music is really great too. The big hit theme song is about finding the light, not being limited by fear, and finding your true self.

You can even take them to this amazing place that also furthered my kids' education and made them even more excited

19 Oxford Reference, s.v. "Wild Man of the Wood," accessed May 17, 2022, https://www.oxfordreference.com/view/10.1093/oi/authority.20110803122507784.

20 *The Son of Bigfoot,* directed by Ben Stassen and Jeremy Degruson (2017; Belgium: nWave Pictures, 2018), DVD.

about Sasquatch: The Sasquatch Outpost in Bailey, Colorado.[21]

Inside they have a scavenger hunt for kids. This is exactly the mentality that should be imbued here. Look around—you never know what you'll find.

As it is with everything, it's about how you position it. It's about perspective.

And above all it's about remaining curious.

Teach your children how to be curious in any way that you can. If you want "smart" kids, this is the foundational ingredient: *teach them how to be curious.*

Go hunting. Go see what you find.

It doesn't matter if you find what you're looking for or not.

What does matter is putting on your adventure hat and going into the woods at all and exploring.

So yeah, *we found Bigfoot.*

Kind of.

21 "Welcome to the Sasquatch Outpost," The Sasquatch Outpost, accessed May 17, 2022, https://www.sasquatchoutpost.com/.

Or you could say that *Bigfoot found us.*

> *"Do we know where the light is the brightest,*
> *Do we know how to clear what the fear is,*
> *Do we know how to feel when we crave it,*
> *Do we know what we are."*

— Puggy, "Where the Light Is" from *The Son of Bigfoot*[22]

---

22 Puggy, vocalist, "Where the Light Is," track 1 from *Son of Bigfoot (Original Motion Picture Soundtrack)*, 2017, digital.

CHAPTER ELEVEN

THE DEEP DIVE

Of all the ideas that we've encountered in our adventures in parenting, general living, or exploring the world, the notion of "deep diving" best encapsulates it all.

Deep diving creates our adventures.

Adventures create deep diving.

I let the kiddos dictate what we explore, for the most part. I'll point and orient and navigate and break apart concepts and interactions. But it's their natural curiosity that pushes us where we need to go.

The analogy is the music we listen to in the car. We listen to a lot of music. Sometimes, I'll hear one of the kiddos singing a song, and even if they don't know the lyrics, I can hear the melody. Or they'll ask to hear a certain song, calling it by what they think a line is saying. Sometimes, I have no idea what they're requesting. Other times, I'll figure it out. And all the time, we listen to *a lot* of the same songs over and over. The kids have them memorized.

Here, they take the lead. They dictate what we dive into and when.

And then we dive as deep as they want to go.

The best dives have been going on for years. Sometimes we surface for a breath and the sun, only to dive back down after some seemingly small spark illuminated the kids' interest in those deep, dark waters of exploration again.

The World Is Watery

Often, even when they express interest in something, it doesn't mean we'll jump into it immediately.

Often, I'm the one who gets excited when they express an interest. I'm the one who wants to dive deep as soon as we can. So, I read them and their interest, because this is about their process, not mine. It's about their excitement, not mine.

I want to reward their curiosity. I never want it to feel like a task.

I never want them to feel as if I saw or heard them express interest in something, and now I'm going to drive them nuts about it and pressure them into exploring it.

I let them drive. I let them lead the dive.

Write It Down—Don't Let It Drown

I keep lists for us of places to go, things to see, and ideas.

And I also make lists of what they've expressed interest in.

So when we have a down moment, a snowy or rainy day, and we're stuck inside, there's no reason to be bored. That's not a word I accept. There's plenty to do. I just go to my lists and start conversations.

Here's our current list:

- Praying mantis
- Corn
- Ghost towns
- Ghosts
- Kid drummers
- Bethany Hamilton, the surfer

- Soccer
- Eardrum eruption
- Types of scientists
- Government
- Satellite dishes
- Dr. Seuss
- Trout
- Trojan horse

Dive. Dive deep. But in order to do so, the only gears you really need are the ability to be a lifelong learner, to remain constantly curious, and to understand how to express your curiosity and listen to the needs and wants of others who want to dive deep.

Go. Be water.

Dive deep. It's the greatest swim you'll ever have.

CHAPTER TWELVE

TAKE A HIKE

I don't like hiking.

   I don't like rock climbing.

So, no, we won't go on a hike or climb a rock.

But ask me to go somewhere.

Ask me to go on an adventure, and I'll start putting on my boots now.

That's the approach I take with the kids: We just say we're going on an adventure. Sure, it'll require walking, probably climbing over a rock, up a hill, scrabbling down a slope, or bushwhacking.

That's exploring.

That's what we do.

If it requires a boat, we'll go back and get one for next time.

If it requires skis, fine. Snowshoes, check.

If I need to reconfigure our gear or procure something else in the mountain-climbing section at REI, I'll do that.

To explain it to others, we'll say things like "We go day camping." But is that even correct? We go out, set up our day tent, eat lunch, and then journey out farther to splash around in the water a little deeper in the interior.

I'm looking forward to colder autumn nights when we can take my stove and some hot chocolate and make s'mores as the sun sets over the Rocky Mountains. What's that called? I have no idea and don't really care.

Just being is like this.

Being just is.

When I'm in my best pocket of life and with the kids, we just are. What we're doing is for somebody else to label if they need to understand.

So thanks, but we probably won't go hiking with you.

We will, however, go on just about any adventure you have in mind.

Do you want to go explore? Perfect, I'll go get the kids' shoes now.

CHAPTER THIRTEEN

THE ADJACENT POSSIBLE

There's no blueprint, in general, on how to be curious about the world and go about exploring and adventuring. One finds the answers alongside their road of simply doing so.

Exploring is one part thinking, two parts doing.

After the gamut has been carefully prepared, as carefully as it can be against the rugged and unsympathetic natural or even human world, adventure is experiential.

> *"The path is made by walking."*
> — Antonio Machado[23]

You'll find all the tools you'll need by walking down the path. If your eyes are open, you'll find them. All the right questions, the correct answers—they're just to your side. All the intellectualizing you'll need to do is included.

One such tool that I stumbled over on my path is a gorgeous concept called the adjacent possible.

Steven Johnson best articulates the adjacent possible: "You begin in a room with four doors, each leading to a new room that you haven't visited yet. Once you open one of those doors and stroll into that

---

23 Antonio Machado, "Traveler, There Is No Path," accessed May 17, 2022, https://www.aspeninstitute.org/wp-content/uploads/2020/04/Machado_Traveler-There-Is-No-Path.pdf.

room, three new doors appear, each leading to a brand-new room that you couldn't have reached from your original starting point."[24]

He goes on, continuing the analogy: "The strange and beautiful truth about the adjacent possible is that its boundaries grow as you explore them. Each new combination opens up the possibility of other new combinations. Think of it as a house that magically expands with each door you open. Keep opening new doors and eventually you'll have built a palace."[25]

I call this combinatorial curiosity. It's long been the cornerstone of my explorations.

And again, I want to make one thing clear: Adventure and exploration do not just have to do with the outside, natural world. This is not just about outfitting a whole expedition to go explore unknown, foreign lands.

I'm much more interested in daily, life-bound, time-bound explorations of our everyday world.

Sometimes it's just about turning down a street and seeing where it takes us. We've actually found new parks, new stream access, even museums—by just driving down a road in our car, in the city, and taking a different road.

This is easier to see out and in the woods. Everything is hidden, around a corner, in the bush, or buried in a forest. You can't quite see everything in the woods, so roads and trails are much more mysterious. The analogy is much clearer where the path ahead is murkier.

Even our consumerism has us immersed in the adjacent possible. At a store once, I saw a piece of turquoise, and a whole new idea, or door, opened up for me: Let's build a family necklace, using turquoise. While searching for the leather and stones and gear to make it, I opened up another door in that room. What did I find? The

---

24 Steven Johnson, *Where Good Ideas Come From: The Natural History of Innovation* (New York: Riverhead Books, 2011), 30–31.

25 Johnson, *Where Good Ideas Come From*, 30–31.

idea of a family crest. So I opened up one of the doors in that room and started playing with virtues and the ideas of what we believe in.

But the greatest journey, the greatest exploration that is being shown to us, is the journey inside. With new disciplines like neuroscience, quantum mechanics, and the growing paradigms in human psychology, for the first time in human history, the inner world is vastly larger than the outer world.

Whichever way, the call is to walk down your path.

Go explore.

Don't worry about what you find. What you'll stumble upon will be greater than what you think

you'll find.

As the Bhagavad Gita tells us so pointedly: "Your commitment is to action alone, not to the fruits of action. That must never be: you must not be motivated by the fruits of your actions."[26]

---

26 "Bhagavad Gita," Humanistic Texts, accessed May 13, 2022, https://www.humanistictexts.org/bhagavad2.htm.

CHAPTER FOURTEEN

CURIOSITY

Curiosity is the cornerstone of cognitive development. Or it should be.

In the traditional canon, it's not.

This has always been very strange to me, that the driving force of our educational paradigm should not be exploration and curiosity. After all, we're all born as meaning-making machines. If you observe an infant and a toddler and most any child, there's an insatiable need for finding explanations for things, for connecting meaning.

"Almost all children ... not only want to know what things are, and
names of things, and simple descriptions,
they want to know why and how.
They have what we call 'epistemic curiosity' —a need to find
explanations for how things work."
— Dr. Susan Engel[27]

It's a shame that our schools believe it to be more important to simply deliver the standard body of information (not knowledge) to our students rather than explicitly teach them how to become lifelong learners.

---

27 "How to Nurture Curious Kids," Early Learning Nation, September 26, 2018, https://earlylearningnation.com/2018/09/how-to-nurture-curious-kids/.

The Family Is the Core

I always leaned toward ideologies that emphasize the individual rather than the group. To this end, I have always believed it was up to someone's family, not just the school system, to truly educate them.

I believe that a truly intelligent, or smart, human is someone who knows a little about a lot. That's somebody who can engage in a conversation with anybody about nearly anything, and although they will not know everything about a certain topic, they can converse about it, both because they know something about the topic, but also because they know nothing about it.

There's courage involved in curiosity.

Being unafraid of not knowing is part of being curious.

In this, education is not simply about facts and figures and grades—it's about a holistic approach. It's about creating individuals who use their whole body and mind to navigate the world. Education is about creating individuals who can succeed as much as they can fail.

Agnosia

The act of knowing is also about the act of unknowing.

It's esoteric, I know.

But not really.

With observation of your cognitive processes, or metacognition, you'll begin to quickly see that what you don't know is equally exciting and present, as present as what you do know.

What is the emotion behind your child asking "Why is the sky blue?"

It's curiosity or intrigue, not fear.

People don't close down when they don't know something. They open up. Or they should, if they were taught with open curiosity.

Not knowing (agnosia) should be taught to be as valuable and inspiring as knowing, if not more so.

Key Words for the Child

Ask

Hunt

Seek

Explore

Examine

Research

Analyze

Inquire

Question

Deconstruct

Key Words for the Parent

Teach

Nourish

Nurture

Lead

Prepare

Instruct

Develop

Guide

Foster

Cultivate

CHAPTER FIFTEEN

ADVERSITY

One of the most important things we can do as parents is to create situations where we voluntarily engage with adversity. This is valuable for our children but also for ourselves.

You don't need to even try very hard, and you'll put your child in adverse situations. Already, their natural curiosity coupled with the unsympathetic universe will put them in difficult positions.

What's important here is to place a mirror in front of us and our children so that they may witness their own courage, especially in the face of failure.

The common act of doing something new will put you in a position to fail. Every new endeavor is most likely an act of failure. And you must be willing to stand in the face of this. As a parent, you must be willing to teach this. In the face of tears, you must be willing to endure the moment and help them move through that emotion.

Handling this adversity, or even discomfort, should stand at the pinnacle of our teachings. It must. It takes a lot to stand in the face of failure. It takes a lot to even be willing to take that risk. To adventure is to risk.

To adventure is to test all the objections that can be presented by the universe. It's a good gauge of whether our teachings hold much water, and whether they are cohesive or not.

And in this, what else happens? You, as a human, singular and apart from your children, create a natural gauntlet for your beliefs, ideologies, and systems. You get to test what you believe. You quickly get to see if what you thought actually holds true.

That gauntlet is the adventure before you.

In order to be the teacher, you must be the student.

The odd thing that happens sometimes is that I'm both, at the same time, with the kids. It can feel like a foolish place to be: Dad is crying, but he's telling everybody to pick up their suffering and turn it into something beautiful. Dad is scared, and they're scared. Dad is the leader, and he needs to get it together and walk forthrightly through this gauntlet here and now to protect us all.

The point is not to lessen fear but to become more courageous.

The point is to help them grow. And in doing that, I have found that I have grown myself. I've forced my own transformation by engaging in these challenges, both large and small. It has forced me to develop, to transform, to challenge old beliefs, by pushing out and into the world.

Growth only happens in that place where chaos meets order. Vygotsky invented and termed it the zone of proximal development (ZPD).

In layman's terms, we call this going into the unknown.

I call this adventuring.

Adversity Grows

What you already know will not make you stronger. But it will make you strong.

Information is to be *in formation*, to be ready.

If you accompany what you have previously won and learned, and you now know what your journey is going to uncover for you down the path, the results can be symphonic.

This is going into the unknown: going places where you do not know everything. And sure, it's uncomfortable. It's supposed to be.

We know this in the same way we know that only when things are messy do we learn or that only when we are challenged do we transform.

And to achieve any of this high-altitude virtue, you must voluntarily put yourself and those around you in challenging situations.

To adventure is to voluntarily put yourself in a place of risk.

Putting my children in the ZPD as much as I can is about positioning my children to be in a place where they can create the skills, both cognitively in problem-solving and emotionally, to prevail in the face of future adversity. (I'm not a madman. I'm not like a boot camp instructor, constantly putting the kids in danger just to grow them—not at all. Rather ZPD comes out in our natural leaning out to explore and discover in the world.)

Adventuring is about creating the character in my children that they'll need to carry themselves forthrightly through the rest of their lives. It's about giving them situations where they can witness their own courage.

I believe it is my primary responsibility as a parent to cultivate the skills necessary in my children so that the social and economic worlds open up to them and they can engage and climb the hierarchies at every level that they will be faced with during their lives.

They remember how tough it was slogging through that wetland. And they still remember that juxtaposition of the beauty and the reward: the way that the creek split into multitudes of directions and the little tumbling shoots back in and under the cottonwoods, through the buckwheat, and in the marshlands. They remember the tiny waterfalls, the quick switchbacks off the main corridor of the wide, sunset creek, and the zillion places everywhere to explore.

And they remember that as much as they remember that Dad forgot the bug repellent and that when we woke up the next morning, they had been bitten to pieces.

I had to face everybody that next day, including their mother, and explain the bites. This led me to humbly create our adventure bag, refine it, and spend time making sure it's complete. This event led me to create a list of critical items to keep in that bag so that, in the chaos of gearing up for an adventure, I already know that what we need is already there, because I check it and replenish supplies in calm times.

Suddenly the teacher was the student again in the ZPD: unafraid, owning it, and transforming with calm fear just as I expect the kids to do when in adversity.

The Three Emotional Tools

One of the most important things we should do to lead and parent our children, our society, is to help create more emotionally endowed people.

Adversity is when we are best given that opportunity.

There are three tools that I've learned about, first used and re-fined on myself, then finally employed with my children. And the tools work. They lead to deeper inquiry methods that saved my life in the darkest of my nights.

All these tools are also great because they can be used on the fly, in a moment when you're transitioning activities or places. They're quick. And they both gain results and create a deeper aptitude in your child.

The Sedona Method

There's a multitude of ways that you can employ this method. I stumbled upon it when I couldn't calm my four-year-old down when he was going through a very dark season.

Again, there are many ways to do this, but this is how we do it.

Me: "You're feeling a big emotion?"

My child nods.

I typically point to their sternum, which is where fear and sad-ness and big emotions constrict.

Me: "Let's take that emotion and put it in a balloon."

Me: "What color balloon do you want to put your emotion in?"

Child: "Red."

I pull my hand away from their sternum in a fist and put the emotion, which I now have in my fist, inside an imaginary balloon.

Me: "Close your eyes and watch that balloon float away from you. It's getting smaller and smaller now, the higher it goes in the sky, away from you. And now ... it's gone."

Me: "See, you let it go. It's all gone."

Physiological Sigh

The physiological sigh is a profound tool that I learned from Dr. Andrew Huberman.[28] His work on neuroscience and brain hacks is truly big, but also practical, stuff.

This sigh was discovered in the 1930s and has been furthered as efficacious in the last decade by researchers at UCLA and Stanford.[29]

Dr. Huberman's big point is twofold: If you want to change how your brain is behaving, you must look to the body to do so—the diaphragm is a great place to do that. Second, this technique helps you get back into the driver's seat of your mind.

The sigh is simple. It is two short inhales followed by a longer exhale. For the two inhales, the first one is typically longer than the second one. The inhales are done through the nose, and the exhale is done through the mouth.

Dr. Huberman's belief is based on current research that says this is the fastest way to bring the autonomic nervous system down in a state of stress. It does so by off-loading as much carbon dioxide as possible—when you do that second short inhale it opens all the little sacks that collapsed in the lungs and fills them with oxygen, letting you better balance the oxygen and carbon dioxide in the bloodstream.

It's a very simple, profound tool that you can use quickly in a moment of haste.

In chapter 17, on happiness, I will discuss the other profound and simple tool that I learned and employ with my children: emotional differentiation.

---

28 "Andrew Huberman, "Reduce Anxiety & Stress with the Physiological Sigh | Huberman Lab Quantal Clip," YouTube, April 7, 2021, video, 2:45, https://www.youtube.com/watch?v=rBdhqBGqiMc.

29 "Use the Breath to Control the Mind," Blue Door Media, accessed May 17, 2022, https://bluedoormedia.co/2021/03/12/using-the-breath-to-control-the-mind.

CHAPTER SIXTEEN

EXPLORATION

The exploratory circuits in our brains are old.

They're as old as anything else in our brain. These circuits are in the oldest part of our brain, in the base of the brain, the hypothalamus.

Exploration is one of our basic behavioral responses.

We get caught up in our daily lives and forget about the simple processes. This is one of the simplest.

Exploring the unknown is designed to make us feel good.

We are meaning-making machines and story-making machines.

Our primary drive is, in my opinion, to search for meaning and to create stories around those morsels of meaning. This is how and why we explore: to find reason, to make reason, to search for reason and life and purpose and goals.

Exploration is in our blood, or in our brain. And it's in the most basic, fundamental, animalistic part of our brain.

Exploring, or going into the unknown, releases dopamine, so it makes us feel good.[30] I think it's fascinating that our brain makes us feel good to crave exploration and then go and do it.

Exploring is also an analgesic, meaning it helps us heal. That's how our brain has prioritized it as a reward.

---

30 "The Science of Curiosity," Britannica Curiosity Compass, accessed May 17, 2022, https://curiosity.britannica.com/science-of-curiosity.html.

Exploring heals.

It's also that primal place where motivation and reward from being motivated have always lived. It's the place where the drive for hunger and thirst lives—the same place where the motivation to explore exists.

Being motivated enough to generate the courage needed to engage in exploring is both the output and the variable needed to make all this happen.

To explore is one of the grand analogies of existence.

It is, at once, motivating and motivation itself.

It feels good.

And it heals.

Caveat Emptor

"Be very, very careful what you put into your head, because you'll never, ever get it out."
— Thomas Cardinal Wolsey

Because we are meaning-making machines and because what we do at all times is create stories around that meaning in order to navigate the world, we must be very careful about which stories we tell our children.

Think about it: Your children may remember a tidbit of information. But what they're more likely to recall is the story of that information if they've tied it to other pieces of information and data they've received and created a story around it.

Creating a story around a concept can be as powerful as experiencing something for a child.

For example, around us, there are hawks everywhere. Sure, I can tell the kids about hawks, show them a picture of a hawk, and point one out when we're walking or in the car. But if I show them a video on sky dancing and how the hawks court, or if I show them another video of hawks circling above a field, looking for prey, then when we're in the woods and they spot that action, the story immediately falls into place. And I know this because it's recounted over and over again—both randomly and when we drive past a field that even looks like the one where we saw that gigantic red-tailed hawk circling because it saw a rodent.

Although I do believe that we should be listening to the children for new ways of perceiving things and remarking on the surprises that they will present us with (a perception like my daughter always saying that the moon is following us all day long), we need to be both active and take care in what stories we give our children.

We need to be vigilant storytellers. We must try to be careful in what we're putting in our children's heads because, if we're wrong in our telling of the tale, it may be difficult to get it out of their heads. But mostly, we always need to be active in telling stories because it's a way to explore the world when we're not even moving through it physically.

Explore.

Moreover, encourage your children to create their own stories about everything, because what this opens up is the drive to explore and create meaning in bits of information and data. And this just may be the goal of all parenting, of all our paradigms: to create healthy, happy, emotionally endowed children who are endowed in those ways because they're curious, they explore, and they're lifelong learners without having to get meta and force it.

CHAPTER SEVENTEEN

HAPPINESS

It's about the path, the journey. I know, you've heard this story already.

But read on: *I bet you haven't.*

It's what research has been saying about happiness: You don't find it in one place. You find it in all kinds of places—because most importantly, you find it along your path. It's not a singular sensation or event or emotion: It's an alloy. It's a compound. It's a synthesis.

It's a process.

There are no things, nor ends, there are only processes and patterns. Everything is in flux, in process. Happiness is one of those processes.

The link between curiosity and happiness is one of the central doctrines that I want my children to understand. And no, it's not because I want them to just be happy.

I want my children to be, if nothing else in this world, *curious.*

If only I would have had eyes explicitly on this prize in my childhood.

In a 2019 study titled "Within-Person Variability in Curiosity During Daily Life and Associations with Well-Being," researchers Lydon-Staley, Zurn, and Bassett explored the correlation between curiosity and well-being.[31]

---

31 Lydon-Staley et al., "Within-Person Variability," 625–641.

What did they find? Curiosity blunts depressed mood and encourages physical activity. In summary, curiosity creates happiness. And happiness creates an ability to be more curious. They go hand in hand.

What does this mean? For me, curiosity is an active function. In order to be curious, one must be in movement. More than that, one must not be afraid of that movement.

What Is Curiosity?

Lydon-Staley, Zurn, and Bassett define curiosity as "the propensity to seek out novel, complex, and challenging interactions with the world. Curiosity facilitates engagement with unfamiliar information, even if that in formation challenges existing beliefs and instills uncertainty."[32]

To be curious is to be active. It's to reach out, with courage, into places and for things that you don't understand.

To be curious is to synthesize. It forces you to face the unknown, to put pieces of a puzzle together in formation, to use the world as parts and parcels of one's informing.

To be curious is to be scared about challenging what you already believe but having enough courage to challenge it anyway.

As is the case with love, being curious isn't a given. In fact, it's not just one thing, one sensation, or one drive. It's a nexus of many different skills.

Being curious means that you will end up in adventurous situations. And with any adventure, built into its etymology, comes the risk of failure.

To be good at being curious you must first be good at failing.

---

32 Lydon-Staley et al., "Within-Person Variability," 625–641.

How to Fail

To be good at failing, you must understand your emotions.

Dr. Todd Kashdan's work emphasizes this with his notion of emotional differentiation. His studies have supported the idea that those who are able to better label and clarify their emotions during a stressful moment are more capable of navigating stressful times.[33]

This means differentiating fear from anxiety, and loneliness from solitude.

This means unraveling subtle emotions.

This means learning how to do this—hopefully, at an early age.

To be good at failing, you must be able to confront and handle confusion and fear. Here, there is a function for negative emotions. Flip them around, and they become our teachers.

When you do this, negative emotions simply become information.

They help us to be in formation.

And if there is one major task we can help our little ones with, so that they can truly, appropriately attempt to accomplish nearly anything, it must be creating emotionally intelligent creatures. Control your emotions, and you can control your actions. Michael Jordan said something similar at his induction to the Basketball Hall of Fame: fear, like limits, is just an illusion.[34]

Emotional differentiation is one of the few tools that I'm aware of that a parent can use on a toddler efficaciously both for long-term growth effects and to create emotionally intelligent adults.

My four-year-old was struggling with his emotions, predictably

33 Todd Kashdan et al., "Unpacking Emotion Differentiation: Transforming Unpleasant Experience by Perceiving Distinctions in Negativity," *Current Directions in Psychological Science* 24, no. 1 (2015): 10-16, https://doi.org/10.1177/0963721414550708.

34 "Michael Jordan: 'Because Limits, Like Fears Are Often Just an Illusion,' Basketball Hall of Fame Induction Speech – 2009," Speakola, accessed May 13, 2022, https://speakola.com/sports/michael-jordan-hall-of-fame-induction-2009.

because of the divorce. When I talked about it with therapists, the idea was this: at his age, there wasn't a ton that could be done. He needed to express his emotions and feel as if he was being heard, but after that, we were a bit at a loss.

Can you believe that less than a hundred years ago we thought that children, toddlers, and babies namely, had nothing of any value to impart to us? We're just now really taking this to heart. But we just don't have that much information about their brains yet.

Using this tool of emotional differentiation in a difficult moment is one way to make sure your child is being heard, but for the long term, it also helps builds this skill of discerning which emotion, exactly, they are feeling.

The practice is simple. Ask the child: "What are you feeling?"

Pause.

Me: "Are you feeling sad?"

A look of inquisition arises on my child's face.

Me: "Is it more like frustration?"

My child's eyes bounce up to mine. "Yes, it's more like frustration."

I typically won't push any further in that moment. But sometimes I will ask, "Do you know why you are feeling that way?" But most of the time I really believe that they just want to be seen. And this accomplishes that.

The more you do it, as an adult, a parent, or a child, the more you can refine and distill and narrow down what the precise, exact emotions are—for you or your child

Truly, it's a lifetime skill.

How to Seek

Believing that "curiosity is the propensity to seek out novel, complex, and challenging interactions with the world"[35] means that one must possess the ability to cope with change, cope with challenges, and cope with a meandering understanding of everything.

The world is in motion. At times it feels like it's not.

At times we feel stuck, even bored.

It's difficult to remember moments of triumph. We most often remember when we failed or when we were hurt. As a parent, I feel the importance of encouraging my kids to remember when they were successful. But I also encourage them to remember that when they were defeated, they were not broken. And when they overcame that despair, I encourage them mostly to think about when they hurdled the obstacle and when they found hidden success.

Dr. Kashdan encourages parents to sit with their children for 10–20 seconds in that kind of moment and to help create those neural pathways so that they'll remember when they prevailed over perceived defeat.[36]

---

35 Lydon-Staley et al., "Within-Person Variability," 625–641.

36 "Professor Todd Kashdan 'The Curiosity Advantage' at Young Minds 2013," YouTube video, 43:44, July 25, 2013, https://youtube.com/watch?v=CzBageKXuys.

When you're more seasoned in tasting moments of defeat, or when your child is, you will build an aptitude, a skill. Couple that with successes and you, or your child, are more apt to engage in adventure, uncertain situations, or novel situations.

When they have the skills, they then create memory to both remember and forget triumphs and tribulations.

And then they're not afraid.

And then they go seeking more.

Before you know it, your child is just naturally, without your push, being curious because they're being brave.

Before you know it, your child is locating novel situations. Not only that, but they are then confronting those situations because they possess the courage to do so. And not only that, but they're also looking for novel situations and confronting them because they have been taught how to handle adversity, whether real or perceived.

Curiosity and Failure

I had a situation with my four-year-old.

Along with his six-year-old sister, who is eight inches taller than him, they attempted a ropes course over a pool. The course used some anchored buoys to transport them across the pool while they held the rope.

My six-year-old succeeded four out of four attempts. She fought and solved angles and fought some more and persisted in ways I didn't know were possible in her. It was really inspiring to see.

But my four-year-old, her brother, couldn't make it. He fell into the water each of his first three times. That third time I could see his dejection, his frustration. My heart was heavy.

I went back with my two-year-old to swim in the lazy river. To my surprise, only a few minutes later I could see Silas standing back up and in line for the ropes course. I was shocked and proud.

I motored through the lazy river and hopped out with his brother. We jumped into the water by the ropes course.

I have never rooted for anybody nor anything harder than I did for Silas in that moment.

He navigated and fought and solved his momentum and angles to get past the first three buoys. He was almost there. Just two more remained.

But alas, he couldn't hold on. He hit the water. When he surfaced, he knew I was right there. I called him over. He was crying. He was spitting mad. I felt as if I wanted to puke. My heart was broken. I was scared because I didn't feel as if I knew what to do to remedy this or make him or me feel better.

Then, right there, as I pulled him in to console him, it hit me: this was exactly what we needed to have happen.

This was not just a learning moment; it was a parenting moment.

"What are you feeling?" I asked. "What emotions, exactly?"

Then, it was my turn. This was a moment to teach him, once again, about adversity—that this is what it feels like to fail, and it really hurts. And remember that pain because it will come again very soon. But we will also remember what happens after this pain recedes, because it will. And we will remember next time when you are tall enough to cross that ropes course and you succeed.

And we will remember that this pain of failing, of losing when we risk, doesn't have to cut so deeply. It is not as strong as we are, because we have practiced. We have learned to trust it and see what magic it creates for us in our life.

We will not live afraid to fail.

We will live to be alive.

Parenting Curiosity

There are multitudes of ways that we, as parents, help our children become more curious. We do it, sometimes, without even thinking. Kids are naturally curious. It's built-in, all the why this and that, all the poking and prodding, and all the doing, even when they're told not to.

But we also inhibit them from becoming fully, independently curious, because we get lazy.

Parenting is a full-time job. It's exhausting. I get it. I've lived it.

But, I believe, it's our responsibility, even when we are tired and do not want to, to create uncertainty. We're not inspired enough to create novel situations. If we can't do that, then we can at least point out the novelties in daily life.

This is to say, point out the subtleties, the nuances, and the things overlooked about the repetitive life.

We believe ourselves to be so aware. Children are actually cocky about this oftentimes. But once you start pointing it out, it quickly becomes evident: We are not very aware at all. We are mostly, or entirely, asleep.

As a parent, I've taken it to be my responsibility to open gaps instead of closing them. Intentionally open those gaps. Intentionally create discomfort.

Evoke curiosity.

Evoke a life well lived.

Parent.

CHAPTER EIGHTEEN

GEOCACHING

Turning the mundane into a pause for magic is the trick of the parent.

Instead of the regular car ride to the store, make a quick stop. Turn the routine ride into a magical memory.

Geocaching is a great tool for creating instant magic.

Of course, you as the parent are already a magician: You can do things your kids can't do. Just opening a tightened jar is wondrous. Coloring inside the lines is a true skill. And getting them home safe after a big, dirty, tiring adventure is the talent of a true magician.

To this end, magic sometimes seems ordinary. But take that ordinariness and transform it into a memory, some meaning, a story. Memories and stories are alchemical. They're magic.

But what's more magical? Cultivating curiosity. And that's exactly what geocaching has helped me to do.

What Is Geocaching?

It's an app-based treasure hunt. You download the app and sign up via Geocaching.com, then you're off. You pull up the map, and you can see all the thousands of caches that have been hidden around you.

There are over a million geocaches on the planet.

The caches range in diversity in the same way that everybody's purposes for caching may vary. There are easy ones. There are very tricky ones. Some are puzzles. Some are just quick grab-and-gos. There are small ones the size of a short bolt. There are big ones like ammo canisters.

For the kids, the bigger ones are better. They have more booty. And that's what the kids want. Sure, they love getting out, and they love the initial thrill of going to find a new cache. But soon the fun wanes when Dad can't find the cache very easily. Still, they hang around, waiting … hoping that there are fun things in the tin box or canister that I'll—hopefully—find.

Whatever you take out of the cache, you must replace it with something of equal or greater value. We carry a cache bag in our car: it's got our head lamps (often we go caching after dark as that's when we have a few hours to get out of the house), and we also have replenishment loot for the caches that we take trinkets from.

You must use the clues granted to you to find the caches. Sometimes the name is a clue. Sometimes there's a hint. Sometimes there's a clue in the description. Because even though each cache has GPS coordinates, often they're off, or even way off.

But even when the GPS is correct, they still can be very difficult to find, like a clever one titled "Barking Up the Right Tree." It had all its bark falling off and piled at its base, but after 30 minutes in the freezing cold, I still couldn't find it. After cutting my ankle up while falling through some wood, we had to call it.

The Thrill

The thrill is in knowing that we're going cache hunting. The thrill is in getting out of the car when you've arrived at the destination.

The thrill is in the exploration.

The thrill is in activating the exploratory circuits in our brains.

It makes you high. (It's dopaminergic.)

It actually helps you heal. (It's analgesic.)

The thrill is in finding the cache.

The thrill is in opening the canister.

The thrill is in examining the trinkets, signing the log, and logging it on the geocaching app.

The thrill is in the ride home, the bonding, the smiles, and the stories.

Our First Cache

So, we decided to hide a cache.

The goal was to take people to our favorite secret places (but not all of them) by hiding caches there.

So, we started with the abandoned grain silo by our house. The idea coalesced very quickly.

I titled it The Gems in the Old Silo.

This cache of gems in the silo was a play on my three kiddos' names: Gemma, Silas, and Harlow.

The hint was that the clues are in the poem.

The cache is on a pulley on the inside of the silo. The canister is attached to a magnet that is attached to a carabiner that is attached to the chain.

The poem

Once there was a boy named Rocketship Joe.
He called himself that, 'cos he lived by this big silo.
Every night he dreamed of flying up to space,
This silo was his ground zero, his rocket base.
The little boy became a man, and grew to become old,
And this was the story he always told:

Search the magnetic cosmos, dream up high,
Though the greatest adventure is inside.
Use your pulley to rope in the tales of the sky,
Until you find your sun, your one, your mind's eye.

The Transformation of Perspective

My four-year-old wanted to hide a cache.

I said, "Absolutely!"

He said that he had a plastic chicken, and that'd work. We were going into a grocery store, and there was an island with some juniper and a light pole. He saw it from the car.

"There," he said. "Let's put the cache there, Dad."

We jumped out, and he proudly put the chicken on the cement base of the light post.

He asked about it for the next couple of days. Then, a week later, he asked about it again. I told him that we were going to that store that day and that we'd check on it. He was excited.

We arrived in the parking lot. I was disappointed to see the chicken still there. But when he saw that it was still in the spot he hid it, he was excited.

"Dad, this is great! It's still here," he exclaimed.

The look on his face brought tears to my eyes.

He had a completely different interpretation of the world. My son and his glowing eyes in that moment were the shiniest part of that day.

Transform the mundane into the spectacular for a child— sometimes it takes less than you think.

Think. Cultivate curiosity.

And voilà! Instant magic.

CHAPTER NINETEEN

WATER

When we have time for an adventure, but I'm not sure where we should go, and the kids don't have an urge for one thing or another, we go to the water.

We go find a lake, a pond, a stream, a creek, or a river.

It was in looking back that I found this idea when recalling our previous adventures: Where did we end up? Most often, by water, or we were motivated by water.

The analogy is almost too saccharine, but it's true: where we once came from and where all life comes from, we must go.

Go to the water.

The analogy is perfect.

Go: Understand how to be water. For a parent, for a human, it may be the most important analogy of them all.

Be water.

Go with the flow.

H 2 Ohhh

The reason why going to water is best for the kids and for me is clear: there's so much for them to do—the flora, the fauna.

We look for toads, frogs, fish, fish fry, crawdads, owls, hawks, coyotes, bears, and moose.

We see bulrush, buckwheat, foxtail, horsetail, cottonwood, poplar, chokecherry, bluebells, golden currant, sumac, and Indian paintbrush.

On the Water

- Go creeking.
- Try to just go from point A to an arbitrary point B.
- Have lunch.
- Bring a snack. Everything tastes better when you've earned it on a hike, on a saunter.
- Watch the sunset.
- Make a campfire, and prepare a snack or meal or hot chocolate.
- Hunt for Asian clamshells.
- Catch toads.
- Look for wildlife.
- Build sand troughs and castles.
- Skip rocks and otherwise throw things in.
- Go in an inflatable raft.
- Sit and listen.
- Stand and watch.
- Just be.

Be Water

Bruce Lee said, "Be water."

It's gorgeous, the quote is.

Especially when coupled with another quote I've long carried with myself:

"There is nothing softer and weaker than water,
And yet there is nothing better for attacking hard and strong things
[…]
All the world knows that the weak over comes the strong and the soft
overcome the hard."
— Lao Tzu[37]

---

37 Wing-tsit Chan, *The Way of Lao Tzu* (New York: Pearson, 1963).

You have to watch the water before you can know how to be like it. You must learn its beauty, and you must learn its horrors. You must learn how to honor it, you must learn how to obey it, and you must learn how to fear it.

Again:

"To understand life is to let yourself be carried away like a cork in a river."
— *Renoir* (2012)[38]

But to understand what it is to go with the current, you must know the difference between the currents: "Son, what is upstream, and which way is downstream? What's the difference between a river and a creek? A lake and a pond? What's a riptide? What is a current at all?"

By the time my children are 10, it is one mission of mine for them to understand, deeply and abstractly, what it means to go with the flow.

Know flow.

Be water.

The Secret Places

We started geocaching, in part, to share with others some of the secret places we've found.

But like any good fly-fishers, we are not that willing to reveal our favorite water places. They're treasures to us. They're discoveries that we won after a long haul, much exploration and maneuvering, and effort, sometimes by accident—most of the time, by accident.

Even when we've been shown a place, or a creek, or another body of water, we find our own nook in that space: our favorite moment in that painting.

---

38 *Renoir,* directed by Gilles Bourdos (2012: France: Mars Distribution).

And so, while we tell others of these magical places, we're not completely willing to let the coordinates out of the bag. After all, these are special places, secret places, or places with few footsteps. On our excursions to these places, we have only spotted a few people ever, which enhances the magic, the cabal.

And so we go, oftentimes, into the unknown to places we've never been or to places we've been to experience it anew, hoping that we'll find a new cove, a new bend, or a new meadow where the sun is perfect on a July afternoon.

The encouragement is precisely the same for you: go find magical places.

Go: be water.

Go: know flow.

CHAPTER TWENTY

TEACH YOUR CHILDREN WELL

I am not that smart. I've long repeated this.

And here in this place where I am a father and a leader and somebody imparting our core philosophy to readers curious about this concept of creative adventuring, it needs to be introduced with clarity:

I'm not that smart.

But I am curious.

For most of my adult life, people have mistaken my sense of curiosity for intelligence. They are often even offended by this in me. They mistake my curiosity for arrogance. But it's simple:

What I don't know, I'll go and research.

What does this mean? For me, for us, for how we live our lives, intelligence isn't the most important and valuable virtue—paying attention is.

This is what I've had to learn on my own, outside of any public education, mentorship, or friendship. This is the golden nugget that I found on my own. And it means everything: paying attention is more important than intellect.

Mr. Know-It-All

Now that we're clear about my intellectual aptitude, let's ask this:

Am I a hypocrite for teaching my kids about standards and concepts that I wasn't aware of in the past but may have only concretized now, while with them?

Absolutely not. This is the highest aim of the parent, in my estimation. This is the sum total of what it means to be a good person and a great parent: the willingness to be humbled by your station in life—both because you can recognize your shortcomings but also because you dare to edit your perspective, own any wrongs, and move forward with more clarity, all on account of effort and humility.

So do I teach my kids everything that I hold myself accountable for as well?

Yes and no.

Some of my foundational ideas weren't made completely explicit until I had to teach one of the kids through a moment. Almost certainly I had an impulsive, pat response. As it was coming out, I would notice what was transpiring and start to immediately question myself: Do I really believe this? Is this true? Is this my idea or something I simply inherited and haven't thought much about?

After spending some time with an idea, and sometimes it calcified rather quickly, especially when talking it through with the kids, the idea became mine and ours and: a standard for myself as well as for the children.

Here, I'm not afraid of being wrong. Discovering that you're wrong about something opens the door to the idea that there are other solutions or that there are better options. That one option or idea that you always thought was the only route? It's not. There's a better route through the Rockies! Hooray!

I am afraid of one thing: of being right.

I think about what I tell the kids. I make sure I believe the same thing. I spend time with the teaching. In part, I want to be wrong, or somewhat wrong. I want to have to explore the idea more.

Being right is boring.

More than that, I don't ever want to be a know-it-all. There are four things I cannot tolerate in a person: selfishness, entitlement, arrogance, and being a cockalorum (which is a know-it-all, something I was forced to find because I was tired of calling somebody around me a clumsy phrase).

These standards have helped me in other arenas of my life: when not around the children, I will often question myself about what the kids would think of my actions, my words, my approach, my resolve, and my motivation.

And so, for what I don't know, I go in search of to solve it.

For what I think I do know, I go in search of to validate it, then edit it. And then I refine it.

So what am I so heatedly in quest of solving? What is the fundamental purpose of all this cause and concern?

Answer: To build a system that will help my kids reveal the best in themselves so that they may compensate when they do err and fall down and fall apart. It is my goal to help them maintain their covenant with the foundation of their earned ideology so that they will triumph when times are darkest and find success even when times are light.

Education

At the heart of our paradigm of creative adventuring is this notion: the public school system and just a singular education paradigm are probably not enough to properly educate children.

How do I know this? Because I experienced it. I studied it.

And now I'm living it.

I will and can teach my children the fundamentals of rote learning, like reading and writing and numbers. But I don't want to spend my days there. I'll let their school and those teachers, with much more commitment and technique, help the kids grow in that way.

For me, education starts and ends at home, with me.

In my opinion, at best, public schools create a factory kind of environment: Sit in rows. Do this now. At the next hour, we switch to this. Jump through this hoop to prove proficiency. And all the teaching is done with a broad stroke, in big classes. Implicit is the notion that this is the curriculum you need to learn, and this is how you're going to do it. This, when students actually have a myriad of manners in which they learn and progress differently.

The phrase "standardized testing" nails this point home.

And that's all fine—to a point.

What this accomplishes is the creation of submissive rule followers. It does not create inspired self-learners. Students under this received model must bring curiosity, like their lunch, to the classroom. This is our responsibility: to understand this and give children a more holistic education.

What is a more holistic education? One that creates curious, lifelong learners. One that creates metacognitive, emotionally endowed adults.

In summary, I believe that the focus in the home should be more about creating curiosity and creating children who are excited to learn and inspired to research. Schools give the kids these tools, but it also only gives them a shallow education. It's our responsibility to demonstrate how the tools they're given in school function in real life and how they can help create a meaningful, happy life.

Unschooling

The worldview that we creative adventurers have created, nay, are constantly creating, is fluid. In a lot of ways, it mirrors the notion of "unschooling."

Unschooling, for me, is a child-led paradigm wherein the children lead the parent, or the teacher, to moments of discovery and teaching.

Children are not robots. Nor are they like the kid sitting next to them in their classroom, however they appear to be topically and on the surface.

Through my undergraduate and graduate studies in philosophy, epistemology, and education, I've long held the notion that curiosity, exploration, and play should be at the core of our teachings, not assembly-line modes of cognition.

If you want inspired kids turned adults, you must facilitate inspiration. You must show them how to be inspired.

If you want interesting adults in our society, you must show them how to be interested.

This is what unschooling is for me: It's exploration. It's practically navigating the world and showing people how to be inspired, how to research, how to be curious about the world, and how to accrue information, knowledge, and then wisdom through experience.

For the most part, at home, the kids lead. This doesn't mean I'm submissive in where we're going—not by any means. Here, I am the curator of their great art museum.

So yes, the kids lead. But mostly, life leads us. It's collaborative. It's a synthesis between us all.

How It Works in the Wild

The creative collaboration and sense of process happen all the time, mostly spontaneously.

One summer day, we walked into a meadow, and my daughter heard a thrumming sound coming from high up in the trees.

"Dad, what is that?"

"That sound?" I responded.

She was silent. Her body said, Yes, that sound.

It was the annual summer sound: that thrumming, a kind of drumming coming from the trees.

"Those are cicadas."

"What are those?" my four-year-old son asked.

"They're these big, ugly, giant insects that come out every summer, and closer to when dusk comes, they make that huge sound."

"I want to see sick-ay-duhs," my son said, phonetically.

I pulled out my phone and showed them a photo of a cicada.

"Eww!" they all three shrieked.

"Yeah, they're a little freaky," I said, wanting to show them their size. "They're bigger than most bugs ..."

Two weeks later we were walking through the forest. And right at my foot in the bulrush, at the base of a cottonwood, was the exoskeleton of a cicada.

I picked it up and asked the kids if they remembered the giant bug sounds coming from the trees.

They nodded.

"This," I showed them, "is how big they are."

"Eww!" they all three shrieked.

And, yes, I learn. I learn with each lesson.

I do not just tell them what I think something is and let it go. Typically, when we're back home I'll look things up to make sure I'm giving them the correct facts. But the kids are young. They probably won't remember everything: in this, I'm actually teaching myself.

One afternoon, we were in a ghost town on the eastern Colorado plains.

We were coming back from examining some abandoned structures, and wading through the turkeyfoot grass, we found something.

"Whoa! It looks like an alien, Dad. Look!"

I took out my camera and snapped a photo.

I didn't know what it was. It did look like an alien.

When we got in the car, I showed the picture to my girlfriend.

"That's a praying mantis," she casually said.

I had no idea what it was. I think I had seen one only once before in a graveyard in Salt Lake City.

Agnosia

I don't know everything. And I don't want to.

I want the world to be a place of exploration and play and adventure. I want my children to live in the same place, where things are wondrous every day and where exploration never ends.

And I want them to live in a place, inside themselves, where they are comfortable coming from a place of unknowing, or of not knowing, because they understand how their world just expanded a little more because there was something new that they didn't know but can come to know.

Learning is exploration. And exploration feels good. It also helps us heal.

This is agnosticism: living in a cloud of unknowing and feeling the wonder and power of one's lack of knowledge, then going after it, sometimes in a counterintuitive manner. Sometimes we go about the quest of quenching that thirst by not explicitly doing anything about it, but instead, we let the world unfold in its organic way before us, without forcing any of it.

Buying into agnosia, for me, is the fuel that ignites the fire of curiosity.

CHAPTER TWENTY ONE

A MINDSET IS FREE

You don't need money to creatively adventure.
To adventure creatively means to turn as many instances as possible into exciting moments of discovery, whether you're on a walk, in the car, on the bus, or on the train.

Creative adventuring is a mindset. More than that, it is the complex wisdom of our old souls telling us that every moment is fleeting, that we should treasure each of those minutes. And more than that, we should expand them like lungs into their fullest breath of being.

You don't need money to do any of that. You just need your mind and the willingness to open it.

I know: Some days or nights you just don't have it in you to get up and out the door with the kids. It's a lot of work, especially when you have three kiddos. But what's more than that, sometimes I just don't know what to do with them.

We rode our bikes yesterday and the day before.

We went to the creek or the beach last night.

So, what do we go do right now that's different or any fun at all?

Do you want to know the easiest way to motivate yourself as a parent? Let the children lead you to the water. Let their enthusiasm and their need for movement and activity lead you. Let them lead you to your adventures, to your explorations, to your discoveries.

And they will, if you listen.

But so will life. Life will also do that for you. Anywhere you are, adventuring is there with you:

"Hey, what's that flower?"

"Did you see that bluebird? What was that? It was really pretty."

"Did you see that critter? I've never seen that around here before."

Creatively adventuring does not mean that you need to get on a plane and go climb Mount Everest. In some ways, that's the antithesis of what the whole paradigm is about.

To creatively adventure means that you let the world open up in front of you, organically.

Here are some activities that I would definitely categorize as creative adventuring. These are activities we've also done and gained a lot from. And they all basically cost little to nothing:

- Making DIY doll clothes
- Painting rocks
- Hunting for heart-shaped rocks
- Catching snails
- Catching toads—frogs vs. toads
- Catching fish
- Catching bugs—buy a bug catcher
- Building a fort
- Backyard camping
- Hunting for herbs and flowers
- Making lilac jelly
- Making cheese
- Filtering water

Embedded in our idea of creatively adventuring is the freest thing you can do: you can also just teach them about things they're interested in.

- Dinosaurs
- Cats: different wild cats in your area
- Dogs: different wild dogs in your area
- Birds: different birds in your area
- Flowers: different flowers in your area
- Bugs: they're everywhere!
- Different types of scientists
- Volcanoes
- Hawaii
- Satellites

Sometimes I'll create a unit study out of something. For example, my four-year-old was interested in volcanoes one day. So, I made a little curriculum out of her proclivity. I springboarded from volcanoes to Hawaii to hula dancers and ukuleles (an instrument we have in our house—this helped couch that for them), etc.

Maybe I'm different from some, but I get energized when we're out and I don't know what something is or exactly how something works, at least not enough to articulate it to the kids. We've all been there:

"Dad, what's that?"

"It's a silo."

"What's a silo?"

"It's a place they store ... grain and things."

"What did they store in that silo?"

"I think they stored grain in there."

"What is grain?"

Go home and research "How do you store grain in a silo?" or "What grains are stored in which silos?"

The first time we saw a bald eagle swoop down by our campsite to snack on a fish, I was stunned. I'd never seen one in the wild, especially in action, that close.

When we returned home, because of my excitement about it all, the kids were intrigued, and what did they want to do as soon as we walked in the door?

"Dad, I want to watch videos about bald eagles."

What this paradigm has taught me more than anything is that—although there is no amelioration for sadness, grief, or a lack of money—trying to expand every moment I have with the kids into something magical is the most honest and noble thing to do, especially when I must overcome life to do so.

But you know what? It's also healing for me.

Some of my favorite moments are when we don't have an agenda or a place to be, but it's just us, all together. This mostly happens in the car when we decide to just take a random turn that turns into a random drive, and then, voilà! We're lost and alone, and it's just us with the windows rolled down at dusk, singing our hearts out to our favorite songs.

When I crave my kids, I often crave these exact moments of freedom and healing.

Adventuring creatively is medicine.

And now because it is just automatic, it is also our life.

CPSIA information can be obtained
at www.ICGtesting.com
Printed in the USA
LVHW082047211022
731269LV00014B/446